PHOTOS: Frank Evers (1), Jörg Lehmann (1), Claude Closky for Jalouse Magazine, Paris (1), Ralph Mecke (1). Cover: Photo von Fargo, Hair & Makeup: Manos c/o Bigoudi, Model: Linda Hardy c/o Next Paris

April 9, 2000
Millennium
Paris
Marathon

May 5, 2000
Seiji Ozawa
conducts the
Boston Sym-
phony Orchestra
and the French
National Orchestra at
an open-air concert on
the Champ de Mars.

June 2000
Johnny Halliday
gives a concert on
the Champs-Elysées.
Free admission!

July 14, 2000
At dusk, the mega-
show "From Lutetia
into the Year 2000"
begins on the Seine.
Plus a colossal fire-
works display!

September 2000
Open-air boxing at the
Eiffel Tower featuring
four world champion-
ship bouts.

September 1–3, 2000
"Festival Seine 2000"
– Paris celebrates its
favorite river.

November 2000
"Discover the Unknown
Paris!" 80 neighbor-
hoods in 20 *arrondis-
sements* introduce
themselves.

They can
go fast:
French francs

Money, s'il vous plaît
Paris is an expensive city. A few tips on managing your personal finances

In the summer of 1999, one U.S. dollar was equivalent to a little over **6 French francs** (FF). If you have a PIN number, you can withdraw money from ATMs around the city. **Plastic** will stand you in good stead in Paris. **Credit cards** are widely accepted, particularly Visa (emergency number if you lose your card: Tel: 01 42 77 11 90) and American Express (Tel: 01 47 77 72 00). But if you want to **change** money, you can do so at countless exchange bureaus (e.g. at the Office du Tourisme, 127, av. des Champs-Elysées, open weekdays, weekends, and on holidays) or at an exchange machine (e.g. at the BRED, 66, av. des Champs-Elysées, 24 hours a day). Two of the city's banks are **open later**: CCF, 115, av. des Champs-Elysées (Mon. through Sat. 9 am–8 pm) and Société Financière de Change, 11, rue Lincoln (Mon. through Fri 10 am–midnight, Sat. and Sun. 10 am–8:30 pm).

Getting to Paris

From the U.S.

Air France now has partnerships with Continental + Delta Airlines, so there are direct flights to Paris from 13 major U.S. cities, including Los Angeles, San Francisco, Chicago, Houston and Miami. There is more choice if you fly out of New York, both in terms of airline and price, including Tower Air, TWA, and United Airlines. U.S. Airways has daily flights from Philadelphia and Pittsburgh.

Courier flights start at around $325, but you have to be flexible about dates and times. The *adventure1.com* website offers a number of flights to Paris.

From the British Isles and Ireland

From London the EuroStar is the most pain-free way of traveling, because it only takes 3 hours to go from downtown London Waterloo to downtown Paris Gare du Nord. Package deals for 2 or more travelers run £59 each. Eurolines offers red hot coach deals at £33 return and a £44 regular fare (on-line booking at *eurolines.co.uk* or call your local National Express). Air France has 18 flights a day from London; British Airways has 16 from Heathrow and 5 from Gatwick. Air France also flies from Edinburgh. Ryanair has direct flights from Glasgow, Dublin and London to Paris-Beauvais. One-way promotional fares run £19.99 (regular £29.99).

1	2	3
4	5	6
7	8	9
*	0	#

Paris Calling

All French phone numbers have 10 digits. Paris numbers begin with 01. If you want to make a call to Paris from your country, dial the international access code, then 33, 1, and followed by the eight-digit number. To make a call outside France from Paris, dial the international access code (00), the country code, the area code (without the 0), and the number. Unfortunately, there are no coin-operated phones left in Paris, so you have to buy a phone card, available at all *tabacs* (tobacco shop) and at post offices.

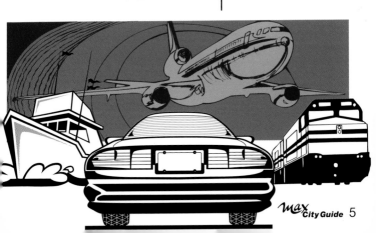

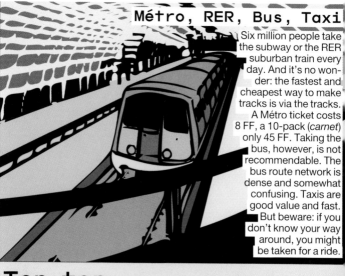

Métro, RER, Bus, Taxi

Six million people take the subway or the RER suburban train every day. And it's no wonder: the fastest and cheapest way to make tracks is via the tracks. A Métro ticket costs 8 FF, a 10-pack (*carnet*) only 45 FF. Taking the bus, however, is not recommendable. The bus route network is dense and somewhat confusing. Taxis are good value and fast. But beware: if you don't know your way around, you might be taken for a ride.

Top ten

No problem filling in the top ten lists.
Paris is a muse

FILM

1. Breathless
Jean-Luc Godard
2. Last Tango in Paris
Bernardo Bertolucci
3. Prêt-à-Porter
Robert Altman
4. Playtime
Jacques Tati
5. The Lovers on the Bridge
Leó Carax
6. The Godson
Jean-Pierre Melville
7. An American in Paris
Vincente Minnelli
8. Subway
Luc Besson
9. Jules and Jim
François Truffaut
10. Zazie
Louis Malle

MUSIC

1. Give Paris One More Chance
Jonathan Richman
2. April In Paris
Tony Bennett
3. Paris s'éveille
Jacques Dutronc
4. Une Nuit à Paris
10cc
5. Our Man In Paris
Dexter Gordon
6. Made In Paris
Trini Lopez
7. Ganz Paris träumt von der Liebe
Caterina Valente
8. Paris, Paris
Malcolm McLaren/
Cathérine Deneuve
9. Bonjour Monsieur
Nina Hagen

LITERATURE

1. Les Enfants Terrible
Jean Cocteau
2. L'Ecume des Jours
Boris Vian
3. Paris, France
Gertrude Stein
4. Swan's Love
Marcel Proust
5. Bel-Ami
Guy de Maupassant
6. The Thief's Journal
Jean Genet
7. Down There
Joris K. Huysmans
8. Thérèse Raquin
Emile Zola
9. Mr. Head
Paul Valéry
10. Zazie dans le Métro
Raymond Queneau

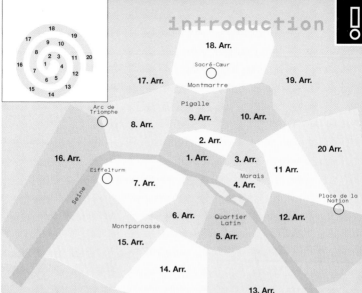

18. Arr.

Sacré-Cœur
Montmartre

17. Arr.   19. Arr.

Pigalle

Arc de
Triomphe

8. Arr.   9. Arr.   10. Arr.

2. Arr.

20 Arr.

16. Arr.   1. Arr.   3. Arr.

Eiffelturm   Marais   11 Arr.

7. Arr.   4. Arr.

Place de la
Nation

6. Arr.   Quartier   12. Arr.
Latin
Montparnasse

15. Arr.   5. Arr.

14. Arr.

13. Arr.

The Big Snail

**Paris' city districts are called *arrondissements*.
To remember where they are, think of Paris as a snail.**

1st arr.: Louvre
Notre Dame is at the center. Otherwise, the Louvre, the Tuileries, and shopping galore.

2nd arr.: Bourse
The financial district. Hopping during the day, quiet at night.

3rd arr.: Temple
The former Jewish quarter: Marais. A great place to stroll and shop.

4th arr.: Hôtel de Ville
This district is dominated by the town hall and the Centre Pompidou.

5th arr.: Panthéon
The intellectual part of town, with the Sorbonne and the Panthéon.

6th arr.: Luxembourg
St.-Germain-des-Prés, no less.

7th arr.: Palais-Bourbon
A residential district of

the "old rich," and, of course, the Eiffel Tower.

8th arr.: Elysée
Center of Paris' east-west axis: the Arc de Triomphe.

9th arr.: Opéra
Pigalle, Moulin Rouge and less stylish establishments.

10th arr.: Enclos-Saint-Laurent
Some residences and the legendary Gare du Nord railway station.

11th arr.: Popincourt
Includes the new Bastille opera, interesting bars + cafès.

12th arr.: Reuilly
Architecturally up-coming since the construction of the Palais Omnisport.

13th arr.: Gobelins
Old workers' quarter, including Chinatown.

14th arr.: Observatoire
Relatively unspectacular residential area.

15th arr.: Vaugirard
The largest and least touristy *arrondissement*.

16th arr.: Passy
Of interest: Bois de Boulogne.

17th arr.: Batignolles
Attractive, quiet residential district.

18th arr.: Butte-Montmartre
Climb up to the Sacré-Cœur and savor the view!

19th arr.: Buttes-Chaumont
Main architectural work: La Villette.

20th arr.: Ménilmontant
Center of young Paris.

Paris in numbers

Population

2.2 million people live within the actual city walls of Paris. Back in 1921, it had over 2.9 million residents. Since then, the populace has spread out all over the metropolitan area, which today has a population of nearly 11 million. The highest population density is 82.5 thousand inhabitants per square mile.

Culture

It's no wonder that other French cities look to the capital with envy. Paris supports more than 160 museums, more than 100 theaters, 670 movie theaters, and over 200 art galleries.

Tourism

Paris has 1,250 hotels and 12 thousand eating establishments. Eight million people flock to the city each year.

The epitome of centralism

Hardly another European capital (with the possible exception of London) stands at the center of its country to such an extent. 70 percent of all large companies are headquartered in Paris; 95 percent of all stocks are bought and sold at the Paris stock exchange; and a quarter of all French civil servants work in the capital.

Help

Police
Tel: 17

Fire department
Sapeurs-Pompiers, also for medical emergencies
Tel: 18

Ambulances for medical emergencies
Tel: 15

Emergency dental treatment
Tel: 01 43 37 51 00
(8 am–10 pm)

Emergency eye treatment
Tel: 01 48 07 22 00
(24 hours)

Night pharmacy
Pharma Presto
Tel: 01 42 42 42 50;
Dérhy/Pharmacie des Champs, 84, av. des Champs-Elysées, 75008
M George V
Tel: 01 45 62 02 41

Psychological problems
SOS Dépression
Tel: 01 45 22 44 44

AIDS help
SIDA Info-Service
Tel: 08 00 84 08 00
(24 hours)

Lost and found
Bureau des Objets Trouvés
36, rue des Morillons, 75015; **M** Convention
Tel: 01 55 76 20 20

American Embassy
2, rue St.-Florentin, 75001; **M** Concorde
Tel: 01 43 12 23 47

British Embassy
35, rue du Fbg. St.-Honoré, 75008
M Madelaine
Tel: 01 44 51 31 00

Literary Paris

What's more Parisian than sitting with a good book in one of the many cozy cafés and drinking one cup of coffee after another? But what book should you read?

Almost every cosmopolitan city honors a famous literary son or daughter. Lübeck, a small city in northern Germany known for its marzipan, pays tribute to Thomas Mann, and the automobile metropolis Detroit pays homage to the great Elmore Leonard.

But no city has been the home of as many major literary figures as Paris: not London, not Berlin, not New York. The list of authors who were inspired by the city on the Seine is long: Djuna Barnes, Walter Benjamin, Julio Cortázar, Ernest Hemingway, Henry Miller, Oscar Wilde, and Marina Zwetajewa...

...Plus the writers hailing from France: the poet Charles Baudelaire, the feminist Simone de Beauvoir, the sensitive Emmanuel Bove, the spiritus rector of surrealism André Breton, the master novelist Louis-Ferdinand Céline, the epic writer Marcel Proust, the jazz trompeter Boris Vian...

But where should one begin? *Paris, France* by Gertrude Stein thrives on repetition and experimentation, so it's not a straightforward guidebook. Nor is *Quiet Days in Clichy* everyone's cup of tea. And James Joyce's *Ulysses* isn't exactly easy reading. You can, however, go to the bookstore that published *Ulysses*: Shakespeare & Company (37, rue de la Bucherie). At this little shop, which is brimming with books, Sylvia Beach published Joyce's masterpiece despite the ban placed on it.

To get a feel for Paris, you might start with the works of Leo Malet.

The author, who died in 1996, wrote more than 40 novels, including a thriller series featuring the detective Nestor Burma, a gregarious anarchist with a caustic sense of humor. Every detective novel takes place in a particular *arrondissement*, and the author describes the socio-cultural millieus of the respective districts capriciously and in a proletarian vein. Along with a map, you can use the book to take a historic tour of Paris.

When Malet was republished in the wake of the '60s revolution, he visited his old stamping grounds. His assessment: "I wasn't able to find much of the poetic landscapes of my youth and the subsequent years. Almost everywhere there are god-damned heaps of glass and concrete!" This is disconcerting to readers. *Mon dieu*, Paris must have been so beautiful back then.

Helmut Ziegler

No budget

Paris is, pardon me, a wickedly expensive city. But there are some exceptions. Here are some of the top free attractions

MUSEUM

Musée du Louvre
Rue du Louvre, 75001
M *Palais-Royale or Musée du Louvre; Tel: 01 40 20 51 51*

The biggest museum in Paris. Free admission from 9 am to 6 pm on the first Sunday of every month.

MOVIES

Cinéma de Plein Air Parc de la Villette
Pelouse du Triangle, Parc de la Villette, 75019; Tel: 01 40 03 76 92

In July and August movies are shown outdoors starting at 10 pm; free admission. Come early or you might have problems finding a place to sit.

CONCERTS

Eglise Saint-Eustache
1, rue Rambuteau, 75001
M *Les Halles*
Tel: 01 42 36 31 05

Excellent organ concerts are held here on Sundays at 5:30 pm. Free admission.

NIGHTLIFE

Le Bus Paladium
6, rue Fontaine, 75009
M *Pigalle*
Tel: 01 53 21 07 33

On Tuesday evenings women get a freebie here. They don't have to pay to get in and they get free drinks to boot.

Le Queen
102, av. des Champs-Elysées 75008; **M** *George V*
Tel: 01 53 89 08 90
Fax: 01 45 61 28 21

On Wednesday evenings free admission for the legendary "Respect" night.

BEAUTY

If you've always dreamed of getting a professional makeup job, go to the perfume department of one of **Paris' large department stores**. One of the cosmetics companies represented there is bound to invite you to have your face done.

PARKS/GARDENS

Jardin des Plantes (Roserai)
Rue Buffon, in front of the Galerie de Minéralogie, 75005; **M** *Gare d'Austerlitz, 7:30 am–5:30 pm (In the summer till 8 pm or sunset)*

Everything you always wanted to know about roses.

SPORTS

La Samaritaine
19, rue de la Monnaie (1st basement), 75001
M *Louvre-Rivoli*

The climbing wall is 16 feet high and 26 feet wide.

Au Vieux Campeur
41, rue des Ecoles, 75005
M *Maubert-Mutualité*
Tel: 01 53 10 48 48

Three-story-high wall with an instructor on Wednesday afternoons.

Organ concerts in Saint-Eustache

Movies in Parc de la Villette

Makeup jobs in department stores

Roses at the Jardin des Plantes

Paris is beautiful

Why people who've seen everything, heard everything, experienced everything – why people like us should go to Paris

You arrived in the city and just drifted around. At first you had a plan, but then you were enveloped by a sea of people – by all the Japanese, Africans, French, English, Swedes, Americans, Brazilians, Australians and Germans. So you decided to just go with the flow, a curious drop in a promising ocean.

You visited the flea market in Clignancourt, watched the sleight-of-hand artists, listened to the singing waitresses at Chez Louisette (130, av. Michelet). You strolled through the Marais, sampled the city's best falafel at Café des Psaumes (14, rue des Rosiers). In Barbès, you pushed your way through a throng of Africans, sauntered through the quaint little streets of Quartier Mouffetard, and had sweet tea and even sweeter pastries in the mosque, blinded by the sun-dazzled marble and the pleasures of the Orient.

You thought the Eiffel Tower was too small (but from the top it seemed high enough), the Louvre boring (but you still got lost), Notre Dame too crowded (but nice), and the Arc de Triomphe rather dull. You ambled down the Champs-Elysées, saw a lousy band in a hall-like bar and a virtuoso saxophone player in a run-down tavern. You had a small, greasy meal at a Chinese greasy-spoon restaurant (not the insider's tip you thought it might be). And finally, you spent your last cash in a mirrored club on a Caipirinha the size of a thimble (but the music was top-notch).

Now it's nighttime. You're sitting on the Pont Neuf. The air is pleasantly cool, the asphalt has finally vaporized the heat of the city and waits exhaustedly for the next day's hot barrage. Below you, the Seine flows coolly and disinterestedly along its empty banks. The trees tremble in a dreamlike state, and even the most valiant buildings have their shutters closed and have retired for the night. The only sound is a distant hum, the breathing of a sleeping city. Paris is beautiful.

The Silly Exposer

A first-rate satire magazine reveals political scandals in France: *Le Canard enchaîné*

No other publication can turn an uninformed tourist into a media insider as quickly as *Le Canard enchaîné*. Of course, you have to be well informed to begin with to know to ask for a copy of the satirical magazine, which comes out on Wednesdays, at a kiosk. The layout is still the way it was back in 1915: no photos, a headline that first-time readers find totally puzzling, strange word plays, and caricatures that are large, small, in boxes, or standing on their own.

At the same time, however, it is one of the most serious and influential French publi-cations. Politicians, business-people, artists – whoever wants to know what's going on in France, what's looming on the horizon, what scandals are brewing, reads the *Canard* (whose name, by the way, de-rives from an old slang expres-sion for newspaper). Despite its irreverent, at times droll tone, this publication has exposed all the biggest political scandals in recent French history.

The second page consists al-most solely of quotes dropped at the periphery of political ac-tivity or in exclusive circles, yet the *Canard* often offers deeper insight than other publications with longer articles. The maga-

zine revealed that the former central African ruler Bokassa gave diamonds as presents to French President Giscard d'Estaing and thus contributed to François Mitterand's victory over d'Estaing in the 1981 elections. And due to the self-aggrandizing attitude of many French politicians, which is conducive to scandals, *Le Canard* is sure to remain successful. So even if your mother tongue isn't French, it's worth trying to read *Le Canard enchaîné*. What's more, with a copy under your arm, you'll be recognized as someone in the know and Parisians might hesitate at taking you for a ride.

Everything daily

A look at Paris' wide range of daily newspapers

Conservative. Both in terms of its political orientation and its focal points: politics, sports, and business. The huge ad section is held in high esteem.

A leftist-center paper for everyone, from brokers to students. It has enjoyed an excellent international reputation since time immemorial, but the staff is having an increasingly hard time living up to it.

Sartre and Simone de Beauvoir were co-founders. In the meantime, it's drifted toward the center, but it's still the main mouthpiece of the leftist intellectual scene.

Who, when, where...

Two paperback-sized magazines (from Wednesday to Tuesday) compete for the edge in informing people about events, times, and venues. The market leader, *pariscope*, costs three francs and is considered to be the Bible of movie listings. The thinner *l'officiel des spectacles* costs only 2.8 Francs, but the flood of information is not as clearly presented.

Lifestyle Galore

No other city in the world produces as many classy magazines as Paris. Here are the best ones

For magazine junkies who love to leaf through shiny, colorful pages, who love to scrutinize the layout, be it rigid or offbeat, become engrossed in the photos and study the texts; who when they go to a new city, even before they have a cup of coffee or have a look around their hotel, make a beeline for the nearest kiosk and scour the magazine section – Paris is a veritable paradise.

1 Jalouse Very elegant. Low-key layout. Lots of fashion, a few portraits, and snippets on culture.
2 WAD Fantastic magazine focusing on skate, hip hop, and street culture. Very reserved, relaxed style. Highly recommended!
3 Self Service Rather arty. Somewhat reminiscent of the British magazine Wallpaper – but without any text.

4 Numéro Extremely ritzy magazine with gobs of fashion and plenty of portraits. Don't be disappointed by the rather conservative layout; the superb photos make up for it.
5 Crash Terrific hip magazine in an unusually handy format. Lots of text, low budget. Captures young French lifestyle.
6 Spoon Only comes out twice a year. Deals with both art and fashion. Lots of great photos, no text.
7 Citizen K Popular, internationally oriented lifestyle magazine covering fashion, design and art, as well as the protagonists in these areas. At the end of the magazine, all of the most important articles are presented in English translation.

The MAX Family

In addition to the parent magazine MAX, two other MAX publications have become established in France: MAX MODE, focusing on men's fashion, and MAX MIXT(E), dealing with general fashion, art, and design.

Name: Radio Nova. Frequency: 101.5 FM. Thanks to a remarkable openness to new pop influences, the station has developed its own style. Playing hip hop, jazz, and a great deal of World Music, Nova is France's most influential young people's station. Rai and rap, daft punk and flat beats – Nova helped these and other types of music become popular. If you want to know what's shaking in Paris, turn the dial to Nova.

www.smartweb. fr/paris
Nicely designed, clearly organized info site on the city.

www.paris.org
Ugly but thorough on-line travel guide. Also in English.

http://mistral.culture. fr/louvre
Tastefully done tour of the Louvre.

Latex Court Jesters

The *guignols* – the bane of French politicians

Parisian hotels that have subscribed to the pay-TV channel *Canal Plus* let their guests know that they can watch soft porn late at night. But you don't have to pay to watch the *guignols*. The favorite show of French youth is shown at the same time as the evening news. *Guignols de l'Info* (in English: "the news clowns") consists of ten-minute satirical sketches on the day's political and social events. The most amusing thing to do is to switch back and forth between the news on TF1 and the *guignols*. On TF1 you might see President Chirac shaking a fellow party member's hand, and the next instant two latex politicians on *Canal Plus* lambasting one another; you see what's going on behind the politicians' routine smiles.

Above the Roof-tops

There are things between heaven and earth that can't be explained – but that can be bought all the same. An unusual look at Parisian design.
Photos by Claude Closky

Fringed leather boots
by Gucci,
on sale at Gucci,
2, rue du Fbg. St.-Honoré,
75008 Paris

of Paris

Skirt with
pillowcase look
by A. F. Vandevorst,
seen at Onward,
147, bd. St.-Germain,
75006 Paris

Paris Designers

Chanel

E 5 *42, av. Montaigne,
75008; Tel: 01 47 23 74 12*
G 5 *31, rue Cambon, 75001*
M *Concorde
Tel: 01 42 86 28 00
Mon. through Sat.
10 am–7 pm
Amex, Visa, Master,
Diners*

Chanel presents prêt-
à-porter collections
from Lagerfeld as
well as cosmetics,
handbags, perfumes,
shoes, and eye-
glasses.

Chloé

G 5 *54–56, rue du Fbg. St.-
Honoré, 75008*
M *Madeleine
Tel: 01 44 94 33 00; Mon.
through Sat. 10 am–7 pm
Visa, Master, Amex, Diners*

For three seasons now,
the fashion world
has been crazy about
Stella McCartney's
collections. You can
ogle her current one
here in a friendly at-
mosphere.

Christian Lacroix

E 4 *73, rue du Fbg. St.-Ho-
noré, 75008;* **M** *St.-Philippe-
du-Roule; Tel: 01 42 68 79 00*
GH 8 *2/4, pl. St.-Sulpice,
75006;* **M** *St.-Sulpice
Tel: 01 46 33 48 95; Mon.
through Sat. 10 am–7 pm
Amex, Visa, Master, Diners*

**Colorful collections:
Christian Lacroix**

Lacroix stands out from
the mainstream. His
multi-colored collec-
tions are chock-full
of pearl embroidery,
appliqués, and unusual
baroque-style matt-
gold accessories.

Christian Dior

G 5 *46, rue du Fbg. St.-
Honoré, 75008*
M *Madeleine
Tel: 01 44 51 55 51*
E 5 *30, av. Montaigne,
75008;* **M** *Franklin Roose-
velt or Alma-Marceau
Tel: 01 40 73 54 44*

*Mon. through Sat.
10 am–7 pm
Amex, Visa, Master, Diners*

Since John Galliano
started designing for
Dior, the prêt-à-porter
collections have become
more trendy. Good
selection. Makeup
service for 350 FF (day),
450 FF (evening).

Jean Paul Gaultier

H 5 *6, rue Vivienne, 75002*
M *Bourse; Tel: 01 42 86 05 05*
K 7 *30, rue du Fbg. St.-
Antoine, 75012;* **M** *Bastille
Tel: 01 44 68 84 84
Mon., Sat. 11 am–7:30 pm,
Tues. through Fri.
10:30 am–7:30 pm
Visa, Master, Amex, Diners*

Both stores sell every-
thing by Gaultier. The
interior of the shop in
the rue Fbg. St.-An-
toine merits a visit:
mosaic floor, tiled
reception area, stars
painted on the ceiling.

Louis Vuitton

D 4 *101, av. des Champs-
Elysées, 75008;* **M** *George V
Tel: 01 53 57 24 00
Mon. through Sat.
10 am–8 pm*
E 5 *54, av. Montaigne,
75008;* **M** *Franklin Roose-
velt; Tel: 01 45 62 47 00
Mon. through Sat.
10 am–7 pm
Amex, Visa, Master, Diners*

**New hip designer:
Louis Vuitton**

For a year now, the
New Yorker Marc
Jacobs has been in

charge of the fashion collections, which are again setting trends.

Junko Shimada

I 6 *54, rue Etienne Marcel, 75002;* **M** *Sentier*
Tel: 01 42 36 36 97
E 5 *40, av. Montaigne, 75008;* **M** *Franklin Roosevelt; Tel: 01 47 23 04 77*
Mon. 12:30 pm–6:30 pm, Tues. through Fri.
9:30 am–6:30 pm, Sat. 10 am–6:30 pm
Visa, Master, Amex

For younger clientele: Junk is loud and colorful

Two boutiques with two concepts. On the av. Montaigne there's the prêt-à-porter collections, shoes and accessories. The second Junk line on the rue Etienne Marcel is for younger people. Loud, but highly wearable fashion.

Prada

G 7 *5, rue de Grenelle, 75006;* **M** *St.-Germain-des-Prés; Tel: 01 45 48 53 14*
D 5 *10, av. Montaigne, 75008;* **M** *Alma-Marceau*
Tel: 01 53 23 99 40
Mon. through Sat.
10 am–7 pm
Visa, Master, Amex, Diners

Spoilt for choice: You can either look around at the three tiny bou-tiques in the rue de Grenelle, or check out all the collections in one store in the av. Montaigne.

Issey Miyake

K 7 *3, pl. des Vosges, 75004;* **M** *Bastille*
Tel: 01 48 87 01 86
Mon. through Sat.
10 am–7 pm
Amex, Visa, Master, Diners

Clothes or works of art? Issey Miyake

Since Issey Miyake's exhibition at the Fondation Cartier, the designer is once again the talk of Paris. His spectacular pieces made of innovative materials are considered minor works of art.

Giorgio Armani

G 5 *6, pl. Vendôme, 75001;* **M** *Opéra or Tuileries*
Tel: 01 42 61 55 09
Mon. through Sat.
10 am–7 pm
Visa, Master, Amex, Diners

Elegant, classical, timeless: Armani is known for the absolute material quality of his creations and for his top-notch styles. At correspondingly high prices, of course.

Barbara Bui

I 6 *23, rue Etienne Marcel, 75001;* **M** *Etienne Marcel*
Tel: 01 40 26 43 65
Mon 1 pm–7:30 pm,

Avant-garde atmosphere: Barbara Bui

Modern ambience: the collection hangs shrink-

Not cheap, but good value: Tati

Tati is not just a place to meet your basic needs. It arouses your desire. All types of consumers are catered to here. In the building for women's clothing there's a floor for overalls and pleated skirts, a floor for disco clothing, a floor for office clothes. The tangas are on a table next to old-fashioned white underwear. Founder Jules Ouaki opened the first Tati back in 1948. Today people from all strata of society buy at Tati, which still has reasonable prices.

I 3 *2–30, bd. Rochechouart, 75018*
M *Barbès; Tel: 01 55 29 50 00*
L 5 *106, rue du Fbg. du Temple, 75011*
M *Belleville; Tel. 01 43 57 92 80*
Mon. through Sat. 10 am–7 pm
Visa, Master, Amex

Shopping arcades

It's raining? No reason to cancel your long-awaited shopping trip. Just go to an arcade

1st **Caroussel du Louvre,** *underground arcade at the Louvre, entrance 89, rue de Rivoli* **M** *Palais-Royal*
Right below the Louvre's entrance pyramid is an underground passageway leading to Paris' newest shopping arcades. Museum boutiques, gift boutiques, and retail chains in an elegant setting.

1st **Galerie Véro-Dodat,** *19, rue Jean-Jacques-Rousseau and 2, rue du Bouloi;* **M** *Palais-Royal*
An old-fashioned arcade with an almost melancholy atmosphere. Next to the shop of the famous doll doctor Robert Capia, you'll find a restaurant, a few art publishers, and some stores specializing in leather goods and glassware.

2nd **Galerie Vivienne,** *rue Vivienne, rue des Petits-Champs;* **M** *Bourse*
The Colbert arcade is regarded as the most elegant arcade in Paris. It was built in 1823, and later opulently restored. Definitely worth seeing is Jean Paul Gaultier's shop and you might want to stop by A Priori Thé where Kenzo, Gaultier and the fashion magazine crowd often drop in.

2nd **Passage du Caire,** *2, pl. du Caire, rue St.-Denis;* **M** *Sentier*

2nd **Passage du Grand Cerf,** *145, rue St.-Denis* **M** *Etienne Marcel*
The land of show-window decorators and prêt-à-porter textile dealers. Two rather inconspicuous arcades in a quarter where confectionary goods are mainly made by people from India. Small red-light district with sex shops and hotels where rooms can be rented by the hour.

9th **Passage Jouffroy,** *10 am–12 noon, bd. Montmartre;* **M** *Rue Montmartre – built in 1846.*

9th **Passage Verdeau,** *6, rue de la Grange-Batelière;* **M** *Rue Montmartre*

9th **Passage des Panoramas,** *11, bd. Montmartre, 10, rue St.-Marc;* **M** *Rue Montmartre*
The arcades are all interconnected and are a must for serious shoppers. Among the magnificent old-fashioned shops such as walking-stick dealers and film poster stores more and more new, youthful shops are opening up.

wrapped in transparent plastic or is laying on white shelves.

Multiple Designers

Kabuki
I 6 *13, rue de Turbigo, 75002;* **M** *Etienne Marcel*
Tel: 01 42 36 44 34
Mon. 1 pm–7:30 pm,
Tues. through Sat.
10:30 am–7:30 pm
Amex, Master, Visa, Diners

Purist design: Kabuki
Very popular shop with Prada, Costume national, Helmut Lang, Martine Sitbon, Dolce & Gabbana and Sergio-Rossi shoes.

Maria Luisa
G 5 *2 + 4, rue Cambon, 75001;* **M** *Concorde*
Tel: 01 47 03 96 15
Mon. through Sat.
10:30 am–7 pm
Visa, Amex, Diners, Master

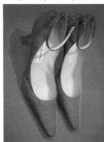

All of Paris lies at her feet: Maria Luisa
Collections by Vande-vorst, Ribiero, West-

wood, and Yamamoto including shoes and handbags. Plus an incredible selection of Manolo Blahnik shoes. Very competent, friendly staff.

Fashion chains

Morgan

G 9 *165, rue de Rennes, 75006;* M *Montparnasse*
Tel: 01 45 48 96 77
G 4 *3, rue du Havre, 75008*
M *St.-Lazare*
Tel: 01 42 93 80 30
Mon. through Sat. 10 am–8 pm
Visa, Master, Amex, Diners

Here you can find everything in vogue at the moment, from evening dresses to stylish trousers. The shops are bright and well organized, the saleswomen friendly and obliging.

Zara

F 8 *59–63, rue de Sèvres, 75016;* M *Sèvres-Babylone*
Tel: 01 45 44 61 60
Mon. through Sat.
10:30 am–7 pm
Visa, Master, Diners, Amex

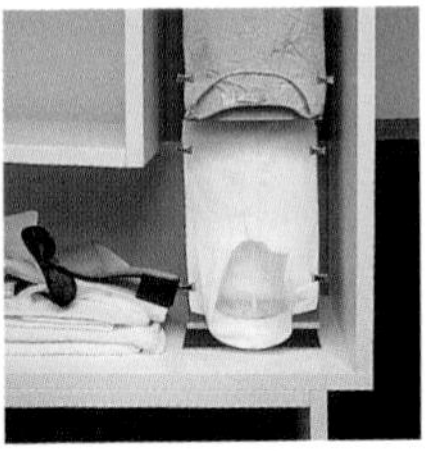

Unemployed PR department: Zara

Modest prices, up-to-date collections, high quality. This clothing chain doesn't need any advertising. It only draws attention to itself twice a year during the *soldes* (sales).

Bargain Shopping

Mouton aux 5 Pattes

G 8 *8 + 10 + 18 + 48, rue St.-Placide, 75006;* M *Sèvres-Babylone or St.-Placide*
Tel: 01 45 48 86 26
Mon. through Sat.
10:30 am–7:30 pm
Visa, Master, Amex

Designer clothing for patient rummagers: Mouton aux 5 Pattes

Prototypes, last year's top-designer collections, overstocks: choice is not what is lacking, and all at bargain-basement prices. "Mouton aux 5 Pattes" is the largest and most well-known *dégriffe* store in Paris. The stock is constantly renewed.

Chercheminippes

G 8 *102–124, rue du Cherche Midi, 75006;* M *Vaneau*
Tel: 01 45 44 97 96
Mon through Sat.
10:30 am–7 pm
Visa, Master

A treasure trove consignment store. Bring in what you don't want to wear any more, provided it's a brand name, a current style, and in perfect condition.

Surplus A.P.C.

G 8 *32, rue Cassette, 75006*
M *Rennes or St.-Placide*
Tel: 01 45 48 43 71
Mon. through Sat. 1 pm–7 pm
Visa, Master, Diners

Select articles from the new and old collections of well-known brands.

Shoes

Karena Schuessler

G 5/6 *264, rue St.-Honoré, 75001;* M *Tuileries*
Tel: 01 53 29 93 93
Mon. through Sat.
10 am–7 pm
Amex, Visa

After her fifth collection, the German designer opened a boutique in Paris in 1998. The interior doesn't draw attention away from her bold soles and heels.

Weston

G 5 *3, bd. de la Madeleine, 75001;* M *Madeleine*
Tel: 01 42 61 11 87
Mon. through Sat. 10 am–7 pm
Visa, Master, Amex

Sur mesure, that is to say, shoes made to measure. Old craftsmanship mixed with new technology. Using state-of-the-art laser technology, a 3D model of the foot is made. The shoes are then handmade in Limoges.

Atelier Mercadale

H 5 *3, place des Victoires, 75001;* M *Sentier or Etienne Marcel; Tel: 01 42 33 86 22*
Mon. through Sat.
10:15 am–7 pm
Amex, Diners, Visa, Master

This shoemaking operation has belonged to the same family for generations. Their specialty: you pick a model, bring the material or leather desired, and the shoes are made right in the workshop.

Michel Perry

H 5 4, rue des Petits-Pères, 75002; **M** Bourse
Tel: 01 42 44 10 07
Mon. through Sat.
10:30 am–7 pm
Amex, Visa, Master

The shoe as a cult object: Michel Perry

In addition to the current Michel Perry collections, this store has models by designers such as Atsuro Tayama, Colette Dinigan, and Kostas Murkudis.

Lingerie

Fifi Chachnil

I 6 68, rue Jean-Jacques Rousseau, 75001; **M** Les Halles; Tel: 01 42 21 37 28
Mon. through Sat.
10 am–7pm
Visa, Amex, Master

First-class *dessous* for soft skin: Chachnil

In the pink boutique you can find first-class clothes for soft skin ranging from silk undies to sequin cocktail dresses.

Sabbia Rosa

G 7 71–73, rue des Saints-Pères, 75006; Tel: 01 45 48 88 37
Mon. through Sat.
10 am–7 pm
Visa, Master, Amex

A master of seduction? But only using natural materials – cotton and a lot of silk. A huge selection of pajamas, nightshirts, slips, and dressing gowns.

Department Stores

Le Bon Marché

G 8 22, rue de Sèvres, 75007
M Sèvres-Babylone
Tel: 01 44 39 80 00
Mon. through Sat.
9:30 am–7 pm
All credit cards

Shopping trendsetter: Le Bon Marché

Le Bon Marché ("good deal") is a historical gem. The largest department store in Paris, it was co-designed by Gustave Eiffel. *La Grande Epicerie*, a food paradise boasting delicacies from all over the world in the second building, is definitely worth seeing.

Le Printemps

G 4 64, bd. Haussmann, 75009; **M** Havre-Caumartin
Tel: 01 42 82 50 00
Mon. through Sat.
9:35 am–7 pm
(Thursdays, nocturne: open till 11 pm)
All credit cards

A mega-store offering everything imaginable in interior design and men's, women's and children's clothing. All the luxury brands, young designers, and bargains too.

Markets
Nowhere else is fresh food revered as much as in Paris

La Samaritaine

H 6 *19, rue de la Monnaie, 75001;* M *Pont-Neuf Tel: 01 40 41 20 20 Mon. through Sat. 9:30 am–7 pm (Thursdays, nocturne: open till 10 pm) All credit cards*

View from Le Toupary restaurant in the Samaritaine

This consumer temple, established in 1870, occupies four buildings. On the fifth floor of the main building is Le Toupary restaurant, affording

a magnificent view of Paris. The sportswear building (no. 3) is especially worth visiting.

Multi-function

Colette

G 5/6 *213, rue St.-Honoré, 75001;* M *Tuileries Tel: 01 55 35 33 90 Mon. through Sat. 10:30 am–7:30 pm Amex, Visa, Diners, Master*

Herds of artworks: Colette

A megastore for art, design, fashion, photography, music, and new technologies. In

the basement is the "water bar" with mineral waters from all over the world.

Killiwatch

Killiwatch: a mecca for secondhand fans

I 6 *64, rue Tiquetonne, 75002;* M *Etienne Marcel Tel: 01 42 21 17 37 Mon. 2 pm–7 pm, Tues., Fri. 11 am–7 pm, Wed., Sat. 10:30 am–7:30 pm All credit cards*

Secondhand selection, streetwear and sportswear. Brands such as

Boulevard Raspail

G 8 *between rue du Cherche-Midi and rue de Rennes, 75006;* M *Rennes Sun. 7 am–1 pm*

Expensive, but very high-quality market. Dealers from all over France sell organic products here. The cheese selection is particularly outstanding.

Le Marché d'Aligre

L 8 *Pl. d'Aligre, 75012;* M *Ledru-Rollin Tues. through Sun. 9:30 am–1 pm*

The cheapest and most pleasant of all of Paris' food markets. Wonderful selection of cheeses. Next door fruit and vegetables displayed like treasures. In the Halle Beauvau pavilion, there are terrific selec-

tions including *le vrai bœuf du Limousin* and *le porc fermier normand élevé en plein air.*

La rue Mouffetard

I 9 *Pl. Monge, 75005;* M *Censier-Daubenton; Tues. through Sun. 8 am–1 pm*

From the south side of the Sainte Geneviève hill, the rue Mouffetard slopes down from the Place de la Contrescarpe toward Les Gobelins. Small streets lined with historic buildings. The street is teeming with food shops and exotic restaurants with large street displays. The flair of a Mediterranean market; high quality, high prices.

Galeries Lafayette
A deparment store like a miniature city. With its own lost and found

Everything that is lost in Paris can be retrieved at the Bureau des Objets Trouvés. At least that's what the guidebooks say. But that's not entirely true. If you leave something at the Galeries Lafayette, you can go to the store's very own lost and found department.

This facility is necessary. Because the department store, which has nine floors plus six annexes – like the even bigger La Samaritaine (between Pont Neuf and 142, rue de Rivoli), whose hardware department would make any hardware chain store manager fall into a deep depression – is as large as a small town. On the children's clothing floor there's a McDonald's, and next to the elegant men's clothes department, a Japanese restaurant. The different levels can be reached by escalator; many of them – as in airports – run horizontally. Galeries Lafayette's reputation is founded, firstly, on the over 75,000 brand-name products sold here, ranging from Benetton to DKNY, from Gap to Kenzo. And secondly, on the occasional bold show-window events, for example the lingerie spectacle, a live show featuring models filing their nails in the bathtub. And thirdly, on the huge *art nouveau* area extending upwards over four floors with a stained-glass cupola and wrought-iron, gilded banisters. However, the higher you climb in the Galeries Lafayette, the shabbier the ceiling, the more you notice just how much plaster has come off. The entrance to the roof terrace doesn't do justice to the view of Paris it affords.

G 4 40, bd. Haussmann, 75009
M Chaussée-d'Antin; Tel. 01 42 82 34 56
Mon. through Sat. 9:30 am–7 pm, Thurs. open till 9 pm
Visa, Master, Amex, Diners

G-Star, Diesel, Buffalo, Calvin Klein. The secondhand articles have been dry-cleaned and are geared to current fashion trends. Speciality: the store's own streetwear brand Killiwatch.

Emporio Armani

GH 7 149, bd. St.-Germain, 75006; **M** St.-Germain-des-Prés; Tel: 01 53 63 33 50
Mon. 11 am–8 pm, Tues. through Sat. 10 am–8 pm
Visa, Master, Amex, Diners

Emporio Armani displays his view of the world on four floors. Fashion for men and women, accessories, CDs, international art and fashion magazines, and select photography books.

Gallery Lagerfeld

H 7/8 40, rue de Seine, 75006; **M** Odéon or Mabillon
Tel: 01 55 42 75 51
Tues. through Sat. 10 am–7 pm
Visa, Master, Amex, Diners

Immerse yourself in the world of the master: Gallery Lagerfeld

Designed by the famous interior designer Andrée Putman,

Karl Lagerfeld gives us a cross-section of his cosmos of taste: fashion, accessories, and perfume. Fans can buy original Lagerfeld photos.

Watches & Jewelry

Swatch Megastore

D 4 *104, av. des Champs-Elysées, 75008*
M *George V*
Tel: 01 56 69 17 00
Mon. through Sat.
10 am–11 pm
Visa, Amex, Master, Diners

Swiss plastic chronometers galore. Playful Swatch watches have long been cult.

KYO

G 7 *32, rue du Dragon, 75006;* M *St.-Germain-des-Prés; Tel: 01 42 22 76 76*
Mon. through Sat.
11 am–7 pm
Amex, Visa, Master, Diners

Timely designs: at KYO

Many watches are imported from Japan and sold here months before they're on sale in normal retail stores. A treasure trove: the

vintage corner, where you can discover interesting models from the 70s.

Cartier

GH 7 *7+23, pl. Vendôme, 75001;* M *Tuileries or Madeleine*
Tel: 01 45 49 65 80
Mon., Sat. 10:30 am–7 pm, Tues. through Fri. 10 am–7 pm
Visa, Master, Amex, Diners

The jewelry legend of Louise Francois Cartier dates back to 1847. A top seller was the "Trinity" ring – three intertwined rings made of three different kinds of gold.

Books

La Hune

GH 7 *170, bd. St.-Germain, 75006;* M *St.-Germain-des-Prés; Tel: 01 45 48 35 85*
Mon. through Sat.
10 am–midnight
All credit cards

Two floors of first-class art volumes, photo books, poetry, and literature.

La Maison de la Presse

I 5 *93, rue Montmartre, 75002;* M *Sentier*
Tel: 01 42 21 46 55
Mon. through Fri.
7:30 am–7 pm, Sat. 9 am–1 pm and 2 pm–6pm
Visa, Amex, Master

Huge selection: Over 2,500 different magazines gleam on the shelves. Plus French bestsellers and numerous guidebooks.

Record Stores

Blue Moon

I 6 *84, rue Quincampoix, 75003;* M *Etienne Marcel*
Tel: 01 40 29 45 60
Mon. through Sat.
11 am–7 pm
Visa, Master

Well-organized vinyl specialist: Blue Moon

All kinds of black music. The focus: reggae imported straight from Jamaica, England, and the U.S.

Crocojazz

I 8 *64, rue de la Montagne-Ste.-Geneviève, 75005*
M *Maubert-Mutualité*
Tel: 01 46 34 78 38;
Tues. through Sat.
11 am–1 pm, 2 pm–7 pm
Visa

Amazingly cheap jazz rarities: Crocojazz

A must for jazz fans! Cheap by Parisian standards. The store has received distinctions several times in *Paris Pas Chère*.

FNAC

I 6 *Forum des Halles – niveau 2, 1, rue Pierre-Lescot, 75001;* M *Les Halles*
Tel: 01 40 41 40 00

Mon. through Sat.
10 am–7 pm
www.fnac.fr
All credit cards

The FNAC chain is an institution in France. A giant selection of music; sells theater and concert tickets to boot.

Food & Drink

Cave Auge

F 4 116, bd. Haussmann, 75008; **M** *St.-Augustin*
Tel: 01 45 22 16 97
Mon. 1 pm–7 pm,

A long date wine dealer with competent staff: Cave Auge

Tues. through Sat.
9 am–7 pm
Visa, Amex

Family-owned since 1850, evident from the antique furnishings matching the fir-green bottle collection. The oldest wine dealer in Paris. Expert awaiting you on two tasting tables, friendly assistance.

Fil'o Fromage

14e 4, rue Poirier-de-Narçay, 75014
M *Pte d'Orléans*
Tel: 01 40 44 86 75
Tues. through Fri.
8:30 am–1:30 pm,
3:30 pm–8 pm,
Sat. 8:30 am–8 pm
Visa

A ten-year old *fromagerie* with an extremely wide selection from all regions of France as well as

other countries. Excellent quality, reasonable prices.

All of Paris loves their cheeses: Fil'o Fromage

Le Fauchon

G 5 26, pl. de la Madeleine, 75008
M *Madeleine*
Tel: 01 47 42 60 11
Mon. through Sat.
9:30 am–7 pm
Visa, Master, Amex, Diners

All kinds of gourmet foods. The *patisserie* is famous for its truffle pralines, an expensive delicacy.

Minimalist fashion from Yamamoto

Shopping Miles

Walks to Parisian consumer temples

1ˢᵗ + 2ⁿᵈ
arrondissements

Rue Etienne Marcel The shopping fun begins right at the Place des Victoires. The historic square, where streets meet to form a star-shaped plaza, is renowned for its good boutiques: Stefan Kélian, Cacharel, Victoire and Plein Sud. Continue down Rue Etienne Marcel to Kenzo and Yohji Yamamoto, and then to Le Shop and across Rue de Louvre back onto Rue Etienne Marcel to Comme des Garçons, Joe & Paul, and Joseph. Check out the kitchen

The *epicerie* has salmon, poultry, game, and liver paté. Large assortment of jams.

Flea markets

Clignancourt

18ᵉ *Les Puces de St.-Ouen, St.-Ouen/Pte de Clignancourt, 75018*
M *Pte de Clignancourt*
Sat. through Mon. 7 am–6 pm (Fri. only for professional buyers)

The oldest, most well-known, and largest Parisian flea market extending over several entire blocks. Vendors sell everything from furniture, dishes, antique jewelry, paintings, sculptures, and books to all kinds of clothing and bizarre hats.

Porte de Vanves

14ᵉ *av. Marc Sangnier + av. Georges Lafenestre*
M *Pte de Vanves*
Sat. and Sun. 8 am–6 pm

Porte de Vanves: haggling over every franc

Around 150 booths selling sheets, tablecloths, dishes, silverware, wooden furniture, old postcards, and books. Many items are sold by numerous professional dealers

directly from small trucks in front of which the best pieces are on display. Don't come too late; the first stands are taken down as early as 1 pm.

Antiques

Fiesta Galerie

J 7 *45, rue Vieille-du-Temple, 75004;* **M** *St.-Paul or Hôtel de Ville*
Tel: 01 42 71 53 34
Tues. through Sat. 12 noon–7 pm, Sun. 2 pm–7 pm
Visa, Master, Diners, Amex

Exquisite selection of American furniture. Creative chaos prevails, but you can find marvelous pieces

accessories at A. Simon and the CDs and books at Killiwatch. Continue toward Rue Tiquetonne, where you'll find some interesting accessories shops, and then turn onto Rue Montorgueil, a market street with nice cafés. Returning to Rue Etienne Marcel, you can have a look at the cheap threads at Naf Naf.

3ʳᵈ+4ᵗʰ arrondissements

Marais The best shopping streets in the Marais are Rue Vieille-du-Temple and rue Francs-Bourgeois. You'll find good boutiques with a diverse selection (clothing, shoes, decorative items, accessories, flowers). Unusual for Paris: many of the shops here are open on Sunday.

6ᵗʰ+7ᵗʰ arrondissement

St.-Germain You could spend days in St.-Germain without walking down the same street twice. A shop here, a boutique there, a nice street café over there. Stroll down the streets around Carrefour de la Croix-Rouge, then head toward Place Saint-Sulpice.

8ᵗʰ arrondissement

Av. Montaigne Devise: pure luxury. Strolling down Av. Montaigne, your eyes will pop out of your head. And on the Champs-Elysées are the famous mega-stores (Fnac, Virgin, Sephora, Disney).

A great collection of Americana: Fiesta Galerie

ranging from cigarette machines to a home bar with stools.

Cosmetics

Sothys Institut de Beauté

FG 5 *128, rue du Fbg. St.-Honoré, 75008*
M *St.-Philippe-du-Roule or Miromesnil*
Tel: 01 53 93 91 53
www.sothys.fr
Mon. through Fri.
10:30 am–22 pm,
Sat 10:30 am–5 pm
Prices: Day makeup 225 FF,
evening makeup 285 FF,
flash de beauté: 40 minutes
for 250 FF, program to
combat skin aging 490 FF,
wax hair removal
50–360 FF,
manicure 190 FF,
pedicure 280 FF
Visa, Amex

For over 50 years, Sothys, an expert in matters of the skin, has been offering a head-to-foot program for the body's largest organ; this consists of algae therapy and a treatment to make the skin firmer. Tip: the *flash beauté*. In 40 minutes, you are refreshed with a massage, body oils, and makeup – preferably right before you go out at night.

Institut de Beauté Revlon

D 4/5 *19, rue de Bassano, 75016;* M *Georges V*
Tel: 01 47 20 05 42
Mon. through Fri.
9:30 am–6:30 pm,
Sat. 10:30 am–5:30 pm
Prices: manicure 195 FF,
wax hair removal 190–250 FF,
facial care 490–990 FF,
body care 490 FF, face lymphatic drainage 490 FF,
body lymphatic drainage 650 FF, hammam 180 FF,
solarium 170 FF
Visa, Master, Diners

In this beauty salon, with new décor and soft light, women are spoiled by experts. Manicures, pedicures, facial care, massage, drainage, wax hair removal, as well as solarium, hammam, and much more. Tip: hand care with peeling.

Institut Lancôme

FG 5 *29, rue du Fbg. St.-Honoré, 75008*
M *Concorde or Madeleine*
Tel: 01 42 65 30 74
Institute: Mon. through Fri. 10 am–8 pm,
Sat. 10 am– 7 pm
Boutique: Mon. through Sat. 10 am–7 pm
Prices: from 200 FF,
day makeup 400 FF,
evening makeup 540 FF,
facial care/massage/self-tanning 100–650 FF,
body care/massage/self-tanning 180–930 FF,
general facial care 450 FF,
general body care 225 FF,
wax hair removal 170–370 FF, stone therapy 670 FF
All credit cards

The moment you receive your welcome

Lancôme: stone therapy for stressed urbanites

drink, you feel you are in the best of hands. A special treat: the stone therapy. Warm stones are laid on and under the oiled body. This stimulates circulation, is good for the skin, and is super-relaxing.

Institut Laugier

17e *39bis, rue Laugier, 75017;* M *Péreire or Ternes*
Tel: 01 42 27 25 03
Tues. through Fri.
9 am–7 pm, Mon.,
Sat. 1 pm–6 pm
Prices: manicure 180 FF,
French manicure 180 FF,
false nails 450 FF
Visa

A "French manicure" transforms natural fingernails by attaching a white capsule to the nail – a nail on a nail, so to speak. Shaped with a special gel and strengthened with a hardening medium, the new fingernail is said to "keep" forever. Robust and attractive.

A little of this, a little of that

Cosmetics is a science in its own right. Here are four experts

Shu Uemura

GH 7 176, bd. St.-Germain, 75006
M St.-Germain-des-Prés
Tel: 01 45 48 02 55
Mon. 11 am–7 pm,
Tues. through Sat. 10 am–7 pm
Visa, Master, Amex, Diners

Giant Japanese cosmetics company. This branch has attentive cosmeticians who all seem to have a sponsoring contract with Issey Miyake.

Annik Goutal

H 8 12, pl. St.-Sulpice, 75006
M St.-Sulpice
Tel: 01 46 33 03 15
Mon. through Sat. 10 am–7 pm
Amex, Visa, Master, Diners

The smallest of the top boutiques has the most charm. In 1986, it was voted best boutique on the left bank.

Sephora

E 5 70, av. des Champs-Elysées, 75008
M Franklin Roosevelt; Tel: 01 53 93 22 50
Mon. through Sat. 10 am–12 midnight,
Sun. and holidays 12 noon–12 midnight
Amex, Visa, Master, Diners

An outstanding perfumery. More than 12 thousand products costing from 3 to 25,000 FF. And the décor of this mega-perfume store is uniquely futuristic.

M.XYT

I 6 11, rue de la Jussienne, 75002
M Etienne Marcel or Les Halles
Tel. 01 42 21 39 80
Mon. through Fri. 10 am–7 pm,
Sat. 12 noon–7 pm; Visa, Master

Very good selection of applicators, brushes, and other makeup accessories. Professional makeup products from Ben Nye, Maquillage, Kryolan, and Serge Louis Alvarez.

New in the program is the *epilation naturelle*, a wax hair removal process using a honey wax which makes the skin especially supple.

Guerlain Institut de Beauté

E 5 68, av. des Champs-Elysées, 75008; **M** Franklin Roosevelt; Tel: 01 45 62 52 57
Mon. through Sat.
9:45 am–7 pm
Prices: makeup from 310 FF, anti-wrinkle program (sometimes for weeks) 720–4,000 FF, face and decolleté 600 FF, manual lymphatic drainage 660 FF, relaxation massage 740 FF, lymphatic drainage 480 FF, wax hair removal 115–430 FF
Visa, Master, Amex

A beauty mission with a lot of style: Guerlain Institute

The Guerlain Institute is one of Paris' historical monuments – with a view of the Champs-Elysées. The individual treatment rooms have been authentically restored and have perfumed name-plates on the door. Little work is done with machines – importance is attached to traditional and professional manual work.

YSL Institut de Beauté

F 4 32, rue du Fbg. St.-Honoré, 75008
M Concorde
Tel: 01 49 24 99 66
Opening hours:
by appointment only
Prices: Acupression 650 FF, decolleté and back 690 FF, slimming 10 treatments 5,400 FF,
manicure from 255 FF, pedicure 360 FF

Men: treatments from 360 to 610 FF
All credit cards

An exclusive beauty institute, almost a beauty farm. Needless to say, products from Yves Saint Laurent are used. In a luxurious atmosphere, you're given personal attention from the very moment you enter.

Hammam

Hammam Med Center

M 2 *43–45, rue Petit, 75019*
M *Ourcq; Tel: 01 42 02 31 05*
Women: Mon. through Fri. 10 am–10 pm, Sun. 10 am–9 pm; men and women: Sat. 10 am–10 pm, admission 130 FF, gommage (entire body peeling) 70 FF, 320 FF lump price with massage and snack in restaurant; Visa

The complete works. In a modern center with a Jacuzzi, sauna, and Moroccan mud treatment, delicious honey pastries are served. The 320 FF for the day includes a little snack at the bar. You are expected to wear a swimming suit, but you can decide for yourself whether you want a henna tattoo (120 FF).

Hammam Oberkampf

KL 6 *160, rue Oberkampf, 75011;* M *Ménilmontant Tel: 01 43 57 67 71*
Daily 11 am–8 pm
No credit cards

A small family-run business with charm. The little swimming pool is supervised. You can get a massage or – by appointment – beauty treatment. The only disadavantage: it can get very crowded. But it's worth the 100 FF entrance fee.

Les Bains du Marais

J 6 *31–33, rue des Blancs-Manteaux, 75004*
M *Hôtel de Ville Tel: 01 44 61 02 02*
Women: Mon. 11 am–8 pm, Tues. 11 am–11 pm, Wed. 11 am–7 pm; men: Thurs. 11 am–11 pm, Fri., Sat. 11 am–8 pm; men and women: Sun. 11 am–11 pm, Wed. 7 pm–midnight Visa, Master

Feel great for 180 FF! Those willing to pay this sum can enjoy an ideal marble hammam with all the extras – massage, epilation, manicure, and pedicure. Towels and sandals are provided. Anti-voyeur measure: on mixed days bathing suits are required.

Hairdressers

Joe Villard Salon / Salon de Couleur

F 7 *55, rue de Bellechasse, 75007;* M *Solférino or Varenne; Tel: 01 45 55 85 69*
Tues. through Sat. 9:30 am–5:30 pm
Closed from August 6–17 Dyeing 270–350 FF, streaking 300–700 FF,
haircut 250 FF
Visa, Master

The master of dyeing, Joe Villard, creates his own colors; they're very natural and don't damage the hair. A small salon with light wood paneling and expert consulting.

Headscape

J 7 *21, rue Vieille-du-Temple, 75004*
M *St.-Paul or Hôtel de Ville Tel: 01 44 61 89 29*
Tues. through Sun. 10 am–9 pm, Sun 2 pm–7 pm; women: around 180 FF; men 140 FF
All credit cards

The art of hairdressing: Headscape

In 300-square-yard surroundings, Arnaud Oyharun opened his first business, a mixture of gallery and hairdresser's salon. In a courtyard in the heart of the Marais is a dynamic team, attractive décor done by California interior designer Peter Steitzner, and great art that changes every three months.

Massato

H 8 *21, rue de Tournon, 75006;* M *Odéon*
Tel: 01 56 24 03 03
Mon. through Sat.
9:30 am–6:30 pm,
Thurs. 11 am–8 pm
Haircut from 460 FF and (from the master himself) 1,000 FF, dying 310 FF
Master, Visa, Amex

Massato is Japanese and has lived in Paris for years now. The fact that he is very busy doing hair for the Parisian fashion scene and haute couture and prêt-à-porter shows doesn't prevent him from running his own salon and often cutting hair there himself.

Space'Hair

IJ 6 *10, rue Rambuteau, 75003;* M *Rambuteau*
Tel: 01 48 87 28 51
Daily 9 am–11 pm,
Mon., Sat. till 10 pm
Classic: Mon. through Sat.
12 noon–8 pm
All credit cards

Hair falls to house music: Space' Hair

For anyone who likes the cliché of the gay, attractive, friendly, competent hairdresser, this is the perfect

place. Listening to terrific house music, you can choose between 300 color shades. If you find it too crowded and the music too heavy, you can try the classical department next door. Prices for a cut start at 195 FF for women and 135 FF for men.

Alexandre Zouari

D 5/6 *1, av. du Président Wilson, 75016*
M *Alma-Marceau*
Tel: 01 47 23 79 00
Mon. through Sat.
9 am–6:30 pm
Visa, Amex

This salon works *sur mesure* (to measure). Haircuts are designed to match the person's face and personality. To have your hair cut and dyed, you have to fork out at least 300 FF; a sitting with extensive consulting starts at 800 FF.

Tattoos & Piercing

Corner

I 6 *131, rue St.-Denis, 75001;* M *Les Halles*
No telephone
Daily 10 am–7 pm
No credit cards

Hidden away in the clothing store is "Cactus: bijou fantaisie, bijou piercing." You can select jewelry for your nose or ear before getting pierced. Price: 70 FF.

Dragon Tattoo

J 7 *5, rue des Mauvais Garçons / rue de la Verrerie, 75004;* M *Hôtel de Ville*
I 6 *12, rue de la Ferronnerie 75001;* M *Châtelet*
Tel: 01 53 40 89 84
Mon. through Sat.
12 noon–8 pm
No credit cards

Both shops offer everything having to do with tattoos starting at 500 FF, including piercing. No need to worry about hygiene – it's very clean.

Absolut Tattoo

H 7 *3, rue André Mazet, 75006;* M *St.-Michel or St.-Germain-des-Prés*
Tel: 01 43 25 40 94
Mon. through Sat.
12 noon–8 pm
Prices: tattoos from 500 FF, piercing from 200 FF
No credit cards

Leaving its mark: Absolut Tattoo

In a little concealed side street, Eric and Kors offer tattoos and piercing: Celtic, Japanese, tribal or custom. They only noses, ears, and stomachs pierce.

The Little

Rai has long moved out of the multicultural niche in French pop culture. One of the singers who played a big role in the boom of this musical style is emerging as a superstar: Faudel

He become a rai singer while sleeping. Or rather, when he was supposed to be sleeping, and while his parents were enjoying a *M'Gille*, the afternoon nap people take in the summer heat in Oran. In these hours between two and four o'clock, Faudel's grandmother passed out tambourines and started singing with her grandson. Songs from her repertoire as a Medehet, a traditional singer who sings at weddings, baptisms, and funerals. When the grandmother wants to hear her grandson sing today, she turns on the TV. With her satellite dish,

she gets all the French channels. Then she calls Faudel and praises him. And she calls often, because it's hard to watch French TV without seeing him. Whether it's a Mother's Day gala or a special with Charles Aznavour – Faudel is always there.

As the first rai star who wasn't born in Algiers or Oran, but in the notorious French suburban of Mantes-la-Jolie, he occupies a unique position in the French music scene, bridging the gap between traditional rai, pop, and *chanson*. He has already become a symbol of the success of

Faudel

Rai is the music of Algerian immigrants. Paris is the center of rai. And Faudel is not only the youngest, but one of the biggest stars of the genre

rince

RAI

North Algerian music, for non-immigrants, and for young people who otherwise listen to Lauryn Hill or Robbie Williams. He started his first band when he was only 12, called "Les Etoiles du Rai." They used the money they earned from concerts at youth centers, wedding receptions, and baptisms to buy better instruments.

These investments were soon to pay off. In December 1996, Faudel signed his first record contract and recorded his successful debut album "Baida." But his major breakthrough came on September 26, 1998. In the giant hall at Bercy, he performed in front of 16,000 people together with the rai stars Rachid Taha and Khaled, accompanied by 63 musicians.

It was not just a musical event, but a social one too – the largest pop concert of 1998 in all of France.

During this event, broadcast live on TV, it became apparent that rai is not just music by Algerians for Algerians, but a driving force in French music as well.

Though Faudel's music has been compared to jazz and reggae, he had a completely different kind of mentor, an internationally acknowledged French singer from an immigrant family who – like Faudel – is not very tall: Charles Aznavour. "He didn't have it easy in life either and sings of love like no other," remarks Faudel respectfully. Faudel says that playing with Aznavour was one of the many incredible strokes of luck in his life. Although he is one of the most easy-going rai singers and does

not view rai as political music, Faudel is still concerned about the plight of young French people from Arab families. He receives many letters in which his fans complain about discrimination, and he knows that racism, for example among doormen at discos, is a daily phenomenon. "When a group of young people who look Arab want to enter a disco, only the girls are let in. The boys have to stay outside," he says in disgust. Faudel wants to be a role model, a locomotive, as he puts it. Nevertheless, he is surrounded by bodyguards at all times. The young singer, popular among all generations, has spawned a strange alliance. Hatred of the young singer has united French racists and Islamic fundamentalists.

Nils Minkmar

Bars

Le Satellit' Café

K 5 *44, rue de la Folie-Méricourt, 75011*
M *Oberkampf*
Tel: 01 47 00 48 87
Tues. through Thurs.
8 pm–3 am,
Fri., Sat. 8 pm–6 am
Visa

Rock around the clock. The owner has over 5,000 records – enough to keep the tunes coming for a long time. The people behind the bar aren't always in the best of moods – perhaps because the clientele drink, rap and boogie till the wee hours of the morning.

Jungle Montmartre

H 2 *32, rue Gabrielle, 75018;* **M** *Abbesses*
Tel: 01 46 06 75 69
Alternating days
11 am–2 am
No credit cards

Friendly bar in a side street in Montmartre. The boss comes from Senegal, as does the music and the reasonably priced, tasty food. The opening hours are flexible.

Chez Richard

J 7 *37, rue Vieille-du-Temple, 75004*
M *Hôtel de Ville*
Tel: 01 42 74 31 65
Daily 5 pm–2 am
Visa, Master

You can lean against the cushy, upholstered leather walls if you start to feel tipsy. Preferably with a Mojito in your hand. Happy hour is from 5 pm to 8:30 pm.

Rosebud

G 9 *11bis, rue Delambre, 75014;* **M** *Vavin*
Tel: 01 43 35 38 54
Daily 7 pm–2 am
Master, Visa

Rosebud: Waiters in white jackets

An American bar with an old-fashioned air. The waiters and barkeepers wear formal white jackets. The clientele is rather set in their ways, but not as stiff as you one might think at first glance.

Tapas

L 7 *17, rue de Lappe, 75011*
M *Bastille*
Tel: 01 43 57 91 12
Mon. through Sat.
7 pm–2 am
Visa, Master

Spanish guitar music. It must be nighttime…

At Tapas, time seems to stand still. Every night (from 10 pm) a guitarist plays flamenco music and Tatiana dances to it. The next time you look at your watch, it's after one in the morning.

Les Couleurs

L 5 *117, rue St.-Maur, 75011;* **M** *Parmentier*
Tel: 01 43 57 95 61
Daily 1 pm–2 am
No credit cards

An offbeat bar in the hip 11th arrondissement. Colorful, smoky, Tom Waits atmosphere. In the heart of the new trendy area around the rue Oberkampf.

L'Oiseau Bariole

J 7 *16, rue Ste.-Croix-de-la-Bretonnerie, 75004*
M *Hôtel de Ville*
Tel: 01 42 72 37 12
Daily 5 pm–5 am
Visa, Master

Traditional watering hole. Not fancy, not trendy – an island in

the *branché* Marais.
A place of refuge for
people who don't want
to be cool. Though the
bar officially closes at
2 am, the party goes
on after the doors are
locked.

Le Comptoir

H 6 *37, rue Berger, 75001*
M *Les Halles*
Tel: 01 40 26 26 66
Mon. through Thurs.
12 am–2 pm,
Fri., Sat. 12 am–3 am
Visa, Master

**Comptoir: World
Music all the way to
the sidewalk**

A chameleon among
Parisian bars. Recently
the décor has taken on
an oriental flair. The
food doesn't change
though, keeping its
Indian touch. Nor does
the music – select
house and World
Music rhythms.

Aux Noctambules

H 3 *24, bd. de Clichy, 75018*
M *Pigalle*
Tel: 01 46 06 16 38
Mon. through Sat.
9 am–4:30 am;
music from 10 pm
Amex, Visa, Master

A quick run-down of
the price system here.
There are three differ-
ent prices for beer. If
you order one at the
bar, it costs 12 FF. If

you have it brought
to the *salon*, you fork
out 18 FF. And if you
order from a waiter
after 10 pm, it sets
you back 25 FF. Many
Parisian bars use this
system. Otherwise,
this singular Pigalle
pub has a conserva-
tive, rocky ambience.

La Fabrique

L 8 *53, rue Fbg. St.-Antoine,*
75011; **M** *Bastille*
Tel: 01 43 07 67 07
Daily 11 am–2 am
Visa

**La Fabrique:
Alsatian flammekueche,
beer, and techno**

The large copper vats
at the entrance tell the
tale: the beer is brewed
on the premises. And
it's a smashing suc-
cess – especially with
younger clientele. The
food is imaginative
and flavorful, particu-
larly the Alsatian-style
flammekueche. The
rather conservative
selection goes ex-
tremely well with
techno and house
music. In the late
hours, people really
boogie down.

Café du Trésor

J 7 *9, rue du Trésor, 75004*
M *Hôtel de Ville or*
Rambuteau
Tel: 01 42 71 78 34
Daily 10 am–2 am
Visa

A meeting spot for
the techno scene. The
most highly touted
Parisian DJs spin for
young techno aficio-
nados, gays from the
Marais, and other
night owls. Everything
is colorful here, in-
cluding the projections.

La Flèche d'Or

20e *102bis, rue de*
Bagnolet, 75020
M *Pte de Bagnolet*
Tel: 01 43 72 04 23
Daily 10 or 11 am–2 am,
sometimes on Mon.
doesn't open till 6 pm
All credit cards

Formerly a stunningly
beautiful railway sta-
tion. Artists and stu-
dents spent years ren-
ovating the building.
Today chic clientele
frequent the establish-
ment. The place has
industrial charm remi-
niscent of Berlin. The
program includes con-
certs, tango evenings
once a week, jazz, and
world music. Sunday
brunch starting at 12
noon.

Man Ray

E 5 *34, rue Marbeuf, 75008*
M *Franklin Roosevelt*
Tel: 01 56 88 36 36
Daily 6 pm–2 am
All credit cards

**Man Ray: a sense of
security while you drink**

Ample space. Different bars with sitting areas and a restaurant.

Word has it that the latter's not so hot. But it's definitely worth having a drink here.

Live Music

Le Bataclan

K 6 *50, bd. Voltaire, 75011*
M *Oberkampf*
Tel: 01 43 14 35 35
*Box office open daily
10:30–7 pm,
concerts from 7:30 pm*
All credit cards

The stage, on which Jane Birkin once made her debut, has lost a little of its magic but is still good enough for top-of-the-line concerts. Sometimes the bill is a mixed bag,

since all kinds of promoters put on concerts here.

La Cigale

I 3 *120, bd. Rochechouart, 75018;* **M** *Pigalle*
Tel: 01 42 23 15 15
Concerts starting at 7 pm
Visa, Master

An old movie theater today used for rock and pop concerts, fashion shows, and performances. The venue can be rented privately.

Divan du Monde

H 3 *75, rue des Martyrs, 75018;* **M** *Pigalle*
Tel: 01 44 92 77 66
*Concerts starting at 7:30 pm,
club from 11:30 pm*
No credit cards

Les Bains Douches

It's no surprise that what was once a favorite among chic clubbers has lost its legendary status

Since the young DJ couple Cathy and David Guetta became the artistic directors two years ago, things have become more democratic in the tiled cellar, at least on weekdays. Younger, multicultural clientele enjoy themselves, say, on soul & funk Wednesday – "Supafly" – or during drum'n'bass day on Sundays, called "Jetvibe." But on the most popular going-out nights, from Thursday to Saturday, the place is predominantly frequented by gentlemen with thinning hair, paunches, and cigars, and slender blond models freshly delivered by the big agencies. On these nights, middle-of-the-road house and hip hop serve as background music. But it's still worth visiting the club today. If you don't mind paying the entrance fee (100 FF on weekdays, 120 FF on weekends), and can afford the drinks (Mojito 90 FF, cola 50 FF), you'll have a lot to see. The floor boasts tile patterns from yesteryear, the heating pipes are exposed in front of red walls, deep-sea fish lie on the bottom of the aquarium, and there are mirrors in the bathrooms.

I 6 *7, rue du Bourg-l'Abbé, 75003;* **M** *Etienne Marcel*
Tel. 01 48 87 01 80; daily 8:30 pm–6 am
Diner 8:30 pm–1 am
Admission 100 FF, Fri., Sat. 120 FF; Visa, Master

Pigalle

From Peep Show to High Culture

In the red-light district, intellectuals have been kissed by the muse for ages. Now the scene itself has a star author: Virginie Despentes

The times when French writers wrote about philosophical issues with elegant fountain pens are over. Following in the footsteps of the successful author Philippe Dijan *(Betty Blue)* was a new generation of men and women authors, some of whom came to literature from very dubious professions. Virginie Despentes, a successful 30-year-old writer who was recently awarded the *Prix de Fleur*, is perhaps the most important representative of this new generation of authors. With a scandalous first work brashly titled *Fuck Me* and then two more novels, almost overnight she became synonomous with a type of tough, straightforward, urban prose that makes Charles Bukowski seem like a children's book author. Despentes worked in Lyon and Paris as a supermarket cashier, a peep show model, and a masseuse before she started to write. For three years, she's been able to live from her new profession.

Her Paris is completely different from the Paris described in "high"

literature. It consists more or less of a small area between the very touristy and expensive Montmartre around the Place du Tertre, where a beer can easily cost 100 francs, Barbès, a quarter inhabited by African and Arab immigrants, and Pigalle, the red-light district and her former place of work. Her neighborhood is one thing above all: loud. "Sometimes the street kids stand on parked cars and

Virginie Despentes: Bukowski is tame by comparison

throw beer cans at one another," she says. Around the rue Poissonière, life is turbulent. Blood from freshly slaughtered lambs

drips onto the floor; loud music is sometimes drowned out by all manner of screaming. For Virginie Despentes, this not only provides inspiration; living there has another advantage. "No one complains when I feel like screaming and throwing things around at night."

It's show time: glamour at the Divan du Monde

Has something for everyone. Black and World Music are particularly in vogue. Sunday evenings, for instance, the group Le Bal gets the place shakin'.

Elysée Montmartre

I 3 *72, bd. Rochechouart, 75018;* **M** *Anvers*
Tel: 01 55 07 06 00
Concerts from 7:30 pm
No credit cards

Concert hall catering mainly to rock and reggae fans. "Scream Night" on Saturdays attracts the gay scene.

Cabaret

Le Paradis Latin

J 8 *28, rue du Cardinal Lemoine, 75005*
M *Cardinal-Lemoine*
Tel: 01 43 25 28 28
Fax: 01 43 29 63 63
Amex, Diners, Master, Visa

The oldest cabaret in Paris, already open back in 1803 under Napoléon. The operators are proud to draw not only Japanese tourists, but many French people as well. Dinner starts at 8 pm, the show at 9:30. Show + dinner costs from 680 FF (including champagne), without dinner 465 FF. Closed on Tuesdays.

Moulin Rouge

G 3 *82, bd. de Clichy, 75018*
M *Blance or Place de Clichy*
Tel: 01 53 09 82 82
Amex, Diners, Master, Visa

Moulin Rouge: the vanes are still turning

Birthplace of cancan and the site of unforgettable performances by such megastars as Edith Piaf, Josephine Baker, Yves Montand, and Frank Sinatra. The show dinner starts at 7 pm, the main event at 9. A tip for newcomers: you can watch the show from the bar and pay only 360 FF. With a bottle of champagne it costs 490 FF and up; with dinner from 770 to 980 FF.

Lido

D 4 *116bis, av. Champs-Elysées, 75008*
M *Georges V*
Tel: 01 40 76 56 10
Fax: 01 45 61 19 41
Amex, Diners, Master, Visa

Lido – a real treat!

Glamour – the word hovers over everything that artists from all over the world present here in shows lasting more than an hour and a half, including flying ballet and figure skating. Needless to say, the prices are glamorous as well. Dinner + show costs 815–1150 FF; show + champagne, 560 FF. The dinner show starts at 8 pm; additional shows at 10 and midnight.

Crazy Horse

D 5 *12, av. Georges-V, 75008;* **M** *Alma-Marceau*
Tel: 01 47 23 32 32
Fax: 01 47 23 48 26
Amex, Master, Visa

Nice bodies, clad only in light, dance on the threshold between art and eroticism, between sadism and humor. Show starts at 8:30 or 11 pm. Price: from 450 FF.

Clubs

La Java

L 5 105, rue du Fbg. du
Temple, 75011
M Belleville
Tel: 01 42 02 20 52
Tues. through Sat.
11 pm–5 am
Admission 80–120 FF
Visa, Master

Not a place to just
stand around. Salsa
and mambo are play-
ed here regularly by
live bands. The club's
not easy to find – you
have to walk down a
former market arcade
to get to it.

VIP Room

D 4 76–78, av. des Champs-
Elysées, 75008
M George V
Tel: 01 56 69 16 66
Tues. through Sun.
11:30 pm–6 am
Visa, Master, Amex,
Diners

**VIP Room: nepotism's
the name of the game**

If you manage to get
past the hulking door-
keeper, you'll get an
exclusive look at an-
other world. The rich
and beautiful let it all
hang out amid red
velvet séparées and
tiger-skin rugs.

Le Cabaret

D 5 68, rue Pierre Charron,
75008; M George V or
Franklin Roosevelt
Tel: 01 42 89 44 14
Mon. through Sat.

11 pm–4 am,
often even later
Free admission: drinks 80
FF, alcohol-free 50 FF.
Visa, Master, Amex

**Le Cabaret: a kiss in
homage…**

Successful mix of
bar and disco. On the
stage, where Edith Piaf
once sang, fashionable
people dance to soul,
funk, and hip hop.
On the last Thursday
of the month: *Soirée
d'Alexi* with well-
known musicians
and DJs.

Dancing de la Coupole

G 9 102, bd. du Montpar-
nasse, 75014; M Vavin
Tel: 01 43 20 14 20
Tues. 9:30 pm–3 am
Admission 100 FF, with
dance course 140 FF
Visa, Master

**Arm in arm: Dancing de
la Coupole**

Tuesday night is salsa
night – terrific atmos-
phere. You can take
lessons at 8:30 pm
and then hit the dance
floor.

Discos

Rex Club

I 5 5, bd. Poissonière, 75002
M Bonne Nouvelle
Tel: 01 42 36 83 98
Wed. through Sat.
11:30 pm–8 am,
closed in August
Admission: 60–80 FF
Visa, Master (admission in
cash only)

Top address for elec-
tronic music. Home
turf of house legend
Laurent Garnier.
Party on weekends;
drum'n'bass or gay
community cool beat
on Thursdays.

**Rex Club: dance till you
drop**

Le Queen

D 4 *102, av. des Champs-Elysées, 75008*
M *George V*
Tel. 01 53 89 08 89
Daily except Wed.
12 midnight–7 am
Admission: 100 FF
Visa

Le Queen: chiseled physiques and wild nights

A gay techno disco par excellence. Pounding rhythms, bodies as attractive as they are sweaty. Great for dance animals, as ceilings are high and you can still breathe in the late morning hours.

Le Gibus

K 5 *18, rue du Fbg. du Temple, 75011*
M *République*
Tel: 01 47 00 78 88
Wed. through Sat. from 12 midnight, open end.
On the last Sunday of the month open from 11:30 pm–12 noon
Admission (Fri. + Sat.) 100 FF
All credit cards

One of the biggest house venues. Hot DJs from London or Detroit are not a rarity here. The interior is pretty cut-and-dry – but who cares when you can dance to the city's finest beats.

Folies Pigalle

H 3 *11, pl. Pigalle, 75018;* **M** *Pigalle*
Tel: 01 48 78 35 56
Daily 11pm–6 am
Admission 40 FF
No credit cards

Folies Pigalle: mint tea and middle-eastern pop

A former cabaret that has lost none of its charm. Rather young clientele, moderate prices. On Sundays there's middle-eastern pop from 5 pm – delicious mint tea is served on the occasion.

The jazz meccas

The Paris jazz scene is among the best in the world. Here are some of the highlights

Petit Journal Montparnasse

F 10 *13, rue du Commandant René Mouchotte, 75014;* **M** *Montparnasse*
Tel: 01 43 21 56 70, Mon. through Sat.
8:30 pm–2 am, concerts from 10 pm
Admission: 100 FF (including a drink)
Amex, Visa, Master

Very popular club. Mainly classical jazz, big band, Dixieland, with a smattering of Latin and R'n'B.

Le Bistrot d'Eustache

I 7 *37, rue Berger, 75001;* **M** *Les Halles*
Tel: 01 40 26 23 20; daily 9:30 am–2 am
Visa

Actually a bistro with traditional French food, but select jazz concerts.

New Morning

I 4 *79, rue des Petites Ecuries, 75010*
M *Château d'Eau; tel: 01 40 25 47 31; Visa*

Jazz, blues, bebop, funk, and Latin, but also African music and ska. Despite the uninteresting concrete decor, it's a warm, homey place with room for up to 500 people.

Le Petit Opportun

I 7 *15, rue des Lavandières Ste.-Opportune, 75001;* **M** *Châtelet*
Tel: 01 42 36 01 36
Tues. through Sat. from 9 pm, closed in August; no credit cards

Small, charming cellar venue with 40 seats and a bar. Bebop and New Orleans jazz are played in an intimate atmosphere.

Show Me!

Who can remember all the tantalizing names the French give to their food? Here's an alternative: pictorial language.

Photos by Frank Evers

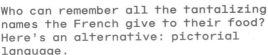

We're all familiar with the situation: a charming restaurant in the heart of Paris, small, discrete, quintessentially French. The friendly waiter hands you two promising menus. But what's this? Everything's in French! And written by hand to boot. And the friendly waiter turns out to be a staunch patriot who would rather bite off his tongue than speak one word of another language. There are two possibilities. You can either stammer and stutter in French, and bear the humiliation, or take out your MAX CITY GUIDE PARIS and triumphantly point to the dish you want. *Voilà!*

Classics

Lipp

GH 7 *151, bd. St.-Germain, 75006*
M *St.-Germain-des-Prés*
Tel: 01 45 48 53 91
Daily 11:30 pm–1 am
Master, Visa, Amex
The food at Lipp reflects Alsatian *joie de vivre*, though the waiters sometimes seem a little stiff and stodgy. Book a table on the ground floor and be prepared for a superb culinary experience. A la carte 250 FF per person.

La Coupole

G 9 *102, bd. du Montparnasse, 75014;* **M** *Vavin*
Tel: 01 43 20 14 20
Daily 11:30 pm–2 am
All credit cards
La Coupole has never gone out of fashion since the heyday of Montparnasse in the 1920s. The big room

A pure delight: seafood at the Coupole

was renovated in 1988 and is now brighter and more attractive. Traditional French fare. The seafood is especially delicious. A la carte 200–250 FF per person.

Le Train Bleu

L 9 *Gare de Lyon, 75012*
M *Gare de Lyon*
Tel: 01 43 43 09 06
Daily 11:30 am–3 pm,
7 pm–2 am, food served
till 11 pm
All credit cards

Le Train Bleu: a feast for the eyes

You shouldn't climb aboard for the food alone. This section of the Gare de Lyon, under a historic preservation order, is above all a treat for the eyes. You can admire the pomp of the Belle Époque. The food is okay – no more and no less. Daily menu at price 150 FF, à la carte 300–350 FF.

Le Pré Catelan

16ᵉ *Bois de Boulogne,*
75016; **M** *Pte Maillot*
Tel: 01 44 14 41 14
Daily 12 noon–2:30 pm,
7 pm–10:30 pm, closed
Sun. evening and Mon.
All credit cards

Le Pré Catelan: Napoleon would've loved it

In the middle of the Bois de Bologne, in a pavilion dating back to the epoch of Napoleon III – as romantic as can be, even for Paris. The chef de cuisine is Frédéric Anton, a disciple of world-famous cook Joël Robuchon. Set price lunch menu starting at 295 FF, evenings from 550 FF.

Le Jules Verne

D 6/7 *2nd floor, Tour Eiffel,*
Champ-de-Mars, 75007
M *Bir-Hakeim*
Tel: 01 45 55 61 44
Daily 12 noon–2 pm,
7:30 pm–10 pm
All credit cards

Half way up the Eiffel Tower is a temple whose 70s décor you will quickly pardon. The food and above all the spectacular view make up for

everything. Even for the bill: the set price lunch menu costs approx. 300 FF, and on evenings expect to dole out around 700 FF per head.

Le Grand Véfour

H 5 *17, rue de Beaujolais,*
75001; **M** *Palais-Royal*
Tel: 01 42 96 56 27
Mon. through Fri.
8 am–1 am,
food 12:30 pm–4:15 pm,
7:30 pm–10:15 pm
All credit cards

2-star deluxe: Le Grand Véfour near the Palais

This restaurant belongs to the Taittinger group, and for this reason alone you can look forward to true elegance. Following a change of owners, the young head chef Guy Martin is preserving the restaurant's excellent reputation. Important: make a reservation well in advance. Fixed lunch menu 360 FF, dinner from 780 FF.

Lo Sushi

DE 4 *8, rue de Berri,*
75008; **M** *George V*
Tel: 01 45 62 01 00
Daily 12 noon–12:30 am
Visa, Master, Amex

Sushi on a conveyor belt: Lo Sushi

The sushi goes round on a conveyor belt. The color of the plates tells you the price. The interior was done by star designer Andrée Putman – everything is ultra-modern and made of glass, wood, and steel. Dishes from 15 to 100 FF.

La Casbah

L 8 18–20, rue Forge Royale, 75011; M Ledru-Rollin; Tel: 01 43 71 10 35
Thurs. through Sat.
9 pm–6 am
Visa, Master, Amex

Sometimes the food's not the main attraction: La Casbah

A modern version of *The Arabian Nights*. Upstairs there's a restaurant with a middle-eastern air; down in the cellar you can dance off the calories in the club.

Le Fumoir

H 6 6, rue Amiral-de-Coligny, 75001; M Louvre
Tel: 01 42 92 00 24
Daily 11 am–2 am
Visa, Master, Amex

Le Fumoir: clientele dressed to the nines

During the big Parisian fashion shows, a meeting place for designers. And the rest of the year, too, Le Fumoir is among Paris' 'in' addresses. Opulent ambience. A la carte approx. 250 FF.

Alcazar

H 7 62, rue Mazarine, 75006; M Odéon
Tel: 01 53 10 19 99
Daily 12 noon–3 pm,
7 pm–1 am
Amex, Visa, Master, Diners

Finer when done by a designer: Conran's Alcazar

Sir Terence Conran's last work in Paris. Needless to say, everything's attractive, light and modern. The food's normally not good value for money. Still, the place is often hopping, especially on Saturday nights. A la carte 320 FF, lunch menu 140–160 FF.

L'Assiette

F 10 181, rue du Château, 75014; M Pernety
Tel: 01 43 22 64 86
Wed. through Sun.
12 noon–2:30 pm,
8 pm–10 pm
Visa, Master

L'Assiette enjoys an excellent reputation, primarily because it was one of Francois Mitterand's favorite restaurants. Cuisine from southwestern France. A la carte approx. 400 FF.

L'Ami Louis

J 5 32, rue du Vertbois, 75003; M Arts et Métiers
Tel: 01 48 87 77 48
Wed. through Sun.
12:15 pm–13:45 pm,
8 pm–11:30 pm,
closed in summer
till August 25
All credit cards

Good food, high-quality meat, large portions. The prices are rather high, but here's a tip: share a dish with someone else. Though it's not the best style, it's tolerated. A la carte 600 FF per person.

The One Star General

In Paris, Chinese food used to be synonomous with greasy egg rolls. Till the celebrated *Guide Michelin* gave Fung Ching Chen a star

What does a cook do if he can't get the ingredients he or she needs? Either he makes do with what is available, or moves someplace else. Fung Ching Chen was not about to make any concessions. "I had a tough time in rural China," he says. "I learned all these elaborate recipes by heart, but all I had to cook with was rice and beans." So he went on a long march. Then talked a border guard into letting him go from mainland China to Hong Kong. That was 27 years ago. He received further training in the British protectorate. Then he went to France – to the El Dorado of gastronomy. "I worked in at least 50 restaurants," Chen says, "before I opened my own in Paris." These days you have to book a table three weeks in advance at Chen's restaurant. And Chen's old ingredient-trauma has been cured. The well-stocked Paris markets offered him every ingredient he had ever dreamt of having, even zucchini blossoms and the white mushrooms that look like roosters' combs. The bountiful supply from all corners of the earth allowed him to try out all the dishes he had learned to make, and set his creative genius into gear. And that gave him such a boost that he became famous. Chen, 48, is the first Chinese chef to receive a Michelin star. "It's a great honor," he says. But cheap food and gluttony never appealed to him to begin with. "Everything has to go together in a dish," he says modestly, "smell, appearance, and taste."

Insider's tips

Café Mosaic

D 5 46, av. George-V, 75008
M *George V*
Tel: 01 47 20 18 09
Daily 8 am–10:30 pm
Visa, Master

Café Mosaic: colorful, usual creations

Chef Paul Pairet has traveled the world and perfected his culinary skills, among other places, in Japan, Australia, and California. As a result, he sometimes concocts very unusual dishes. The establishment is not just a feast for the stomach, but also for the eyes. Approx. 250 FF per person.

Au Camelot

K 7 50, rue Amelot, 75011
M *Chemin Vert*
Tel: 01 43 55 54 04
Tues. through Sat.
12 noon–2 pm, 7 pm–11 pm
(Sat. till 1 am); Visa, Master

Au Camelot: sometimes less feels like more

Dining around the world

Variety is the spice of life. And restaurants of all nationalities are the spice of Paris. A look at international cuisine in the city

North African

Chez Omar

*JK 6 47, rue de Bretagne,
75003; M République
Tel: 01 42 72 36 26
Mon. through Sat.
12 noon–3 pm, 6–12 pm
Visa, Master*

It's said there are
people who don't know
what couscous is.
Omar can educate
them, heartily and
affordably.

Indian

Ville de Jagannath

*L 5/6 101, rue St.-Maur,
75011; M St.-Maur
Tel: 01 43 55 80 81
Mon. through Thurs.
7:30–10:30 pm,
Fri, Sat. 7:30 pm –12:30 am
Visa*

No place for sinners.
There's a corner for
smokers, but otherwise
it's non-smoking. And
strictly vegetarian.

Yiddish

Chez Marianne

*J 7 2, rue des Hospitalières-
St-Gervais, 75004; M St-Paul
Tel: 01 42 72 18 86
Daily 11 am–12 pm
Visa, Master*

Yiddish-Eastern-Euro-
pean cuisine. Dishes
ranging from sweet
strudel to eggplant
purée and humus.

Argentinian

Anahi

*J 5 49, rue Volta, 75003
M Arts et Métiers
Tel: 01 48 87 88 24
Daily 10–2 am
Visa, Master*

Top-quality beef, fresh
salads, fish marinat-
ed in coriander, and
choice South American
wines.

Spanish

Fogon Saint-Julien

*I 8 10, rue St.-Julien-le-
Pauvre, 75005
M St.-Michel
Tel: 01 43 54 31 33
Daily 12 am–3:30 pm,
8 pm–2 am, food till 12:30 pm
Visa, Master*

Nice atmosphere in a
half-timbered building.
Excellent squid and
delicious rice with
fresh cod and raisins.

Scandinavian

Café des Lettres

*G 7 53, rue de Verneuil,
75007; M Rue du Bac
Tel: 01 42 22 52 17;
Mon. through Fri.
9 am–11 pm,
Sat. 11 am–11 pm,
Sun. 12 am–4 pm
Visa, Master*

A popular meeting
spot for the literary
scene. Hearty, meaty
fare.

Excellent food at
affordable prices.
There's just one dinner
menu. The restaurant
only has 40 seats, so
book in advance.
Fixed price lunch
menu 140 FF, dinner
with wine approx.
160 FF per person.

Café Foy

*H 6 165, rue St.-Honoré,
75001; M Louvre or Palais
Royal; Tel: 01 42 86 06 96
Daily 9 am–2 pm,
food till midnight
All credit cards*

**The Foy combines
tasty morsels and
literature**

Almost a literary café/
restaurant. Every
Thursday informal
literary events. Tradi-
tional French fare
with exotic nuances
and spices. Menu
124 FF, lunch menu
100 FF, à la carte
200–250 FF.

Wine bars

La Tartine

*J 7 24, rue de Rivoli,
75004; M St.-Paul
Tel: 01 42 72 76 85
Daily 8 am–10:30 pm,
Closed Tues., Wed.
mornings
No credit cards*

Tartine: where time stands still

A legend getting on in years. The walls are yellow from millions of Gauloises, and the service has seen better days. Sipping a glass of wine, people watch time stand still. And occasionally have a look at the *Le Monde* newspaper – to see what year it is.

Le Baron Rouge

L 8 *1, rue Théophile Roussel, 75012*
M *Ledru-Rollin*
Tel: 01 43 42 54 65
Tues. through Thurs.
10 am–2 pm, 5 pm–10 pm,
Fri., Sat. 10 am–10 pm,
Sun. 10 am–4 pm
Visa

Le Baron Rouge: wine for every occasion

The red baron beckons you to try a wine of the same color. And since it only costs

from 12 to 17 FF, and the cheese or sausage plate only 30 FF, the red baron is very popular. Every Sunday morning, fresh oysters.

Taverne Henri IV

H 7 *13, pl. du Pont-Neuf, 75001;* **M** *Pont-Neuf*
Tel: 01 43 54 27 90
Mon. through Fri.
12 noon–8:30 pm,
Sat. 12 noon–4 pm,
closed in August
No credit cards

Henri IV: wines from all over the world

Likely the city's oldest wine tavern. Large selection of wines from all regions. Tartines to eat. The building alone, from the era of Louis XIII, is an experience. Unfortunately many tourists feel the same way, and it's almost always packed.

Asian

Higuma

H 5 *32, rue Ste.-Anne, 75002;* **M** *Pyramides*
Tel: 01 47 03 38 59
Daily 11:30 am–10 pm
Visa

Culinary insight: a peek in the pots at Higuma

A soup lover's paradise. Because here they serve all kinds of Japanese soups. A real treat: sit at the counter and watch the cooks and waiters in action. Approx. 70 FF per person.

Dave

G 5 *39, rue St.-Roch, 75001*
M *Pyramides*
Tel: 01 42 61 49 48
Daily 12 noon–2:30 pm,
closed Sat., Sun.
afternoons
All credit cards

An institution. This Chinese restaurant has been a hot spot for the Parisian fashion world for years now. Chef Dave likes to point out that five generations of models have frequented his eating establishment. The food is Chinese with a European bent and costs 200–250 FF per person.

Isse

H 5 *56, rue Ste.-Anne, 75002;* **M** *Pyramides*
Tel: 01 42 96 67 76
Tues. through Fri.
12 noon–2 pm,
7 pm–10 pm,
Mon., Sat. 12 noon–10 pm
Visa, Master

Isse: Japanese food for Japanese people – and the rest of the world

Many Japanese businesspeople munch here. The food is delicious – and wickedly expensive. The lunch menu costs around 350 FF, dinner easily twice as expensive.

Italian

Enzo

G 11 *59, rue Daguerre, 75014;* M *Denfert-Rochereau; Tel: 01 43 21 66 66*
Mon. through Fri.
2 noon–3 pm,
Mon. through Sat.
6:30 pm–11 pm
All credit cards

Enzo: a very small place, but with very tasty food

To eat at Enzo you have to make a reservation and be on time. Otherwise you don't stand a chance of getting one of the ten seats. The spaghetti and pizza are cheap and delicious.

Il Barone

G 9 *7, rue Léopold Robert 75014;* M *Vavin*
Tel: 01 43 20 87 14
Mon. through Sat.
12 noon–3 pm, daily
7 pm– midnight
Visa, Master

The epitome of a good Italian restaurant. The pasta is homemade. Now and then celebrities dine here – in part because they're left in peace and because all customers are treated equally. A la carte 200–250 FF. Definitely make reservations on weekends.

Da Mimmo

J 4 *39, bd. de Magenta, 75010* M *Gare de L'Est*
Tel: 01 42 06 44 47
Mon. through Sat.
12 noon– 2:30 pm, 7 pm–11:30 pm, closed in August
Visa, Master

This is the home of the most delicious arugula pizza in Paris. The waiters are sometimes a little too cocky. From 200 FF per person.

Mid price

Le Petit Bofinger

K 7 *6, rue de la Bastille, 75004;* M *Bastille*
Tel: 01 42 72 05 23
Daily 12 noon–3 pm,
7 pm– midnight
Visa, Master

More relaxed than its brother: Petit Bofinger

The Great Outdoors

Nice places to have *café au lait* outside

Au Père tranquille

I 6 *16, rue Pierre Lescot, 75001;* M *Les Halles*
Tel. 01 45 08 00 34
Daily 8 am–2 pm
Visa, Master

The "tranquil father" isn't exactly cheap and is often full of tourists. Still, the bistro is one of the most popular outdoor cafés in the Les Halles district. There's a lot to admire here – not least the waiters rushing back and forth. *Café au lait* 24 FF.

The little brother of the famous *brasserie*. The ambience is sophisticated, but not as beautiful-people posh as in the main restaurant across the way. Recommendations: *pot au feu, foie gras de canard maison*. Approx. 150–200 FF per person.

Bistro de l'Huitre

H 9 *285, rue St.-Jacques, 75005;* **M** *Port Royal Tel: 01 43 54 71 70 Tues. through Sat. 10:30 am–2 pm, 6:30 pm–11:30 pm Visa, Master*

Housed in a former butcher's shop. But the days of meaty glory are gone: the bistro has exclusively fish

and seafood on the menu. There are only 26 seats, so definitely book a table.

Le Bar à Huitre

G 9 *112, bd. du Montparnasse, 75014;* **M** *Vavin Tel: 01 43 20 71 01 Daily 12 noon–2 pm All credit cards*

Seafood galore: Le Bar à Huitre

Oysters and seafood – two reasons to eat at Le Bar à Huitre. And in the fall there are scallops in fennel butter – simply delicious! A la carte approx. 220 FF, fixed menu 100–200 FF.

Good deal

L'Encrier

L 9 *55, rue Traversière, 75012;* **M** *Gare de Lyon Tel: 01 44 68 08 16 Mon. through Fri. 12 noon– 2:15 pm, 7:15 pm–11 pm, Sat. 7:15 pm–11pm Visa, Master*

Charming little bistro. Excellent food and wines for little money. Sometimes the wait is too long – but it's worth it. A la carte 100 FF per person.

Café de la Mairie

G 8 *8, pl. St.-Sulpice, 75006* **M** *St.-Sulpice Tel. 01 43 26 67 82 Mon. through Sat. 7 am– 2 pm; no credit cards*

Plain café that thrives on its reputation. In summer the terrace is almost always jam-packed. *Café au lait* 20 FF, beer 20 FF, food from 45 FF.

L'Eté En Pente Douce

H I *23, rue Muller, 75018* **M** *Abbesses or Château Rouge; Tel. 01 42 64 02 67 Daily 12 noon–24 pm Visa, Master*

Tea salon, ice-cream parlor and restaurant

all in one. About half way up the hill to Sacré-Cœur.

Le Rendez-vous des Quais

J 7 *10, quai de la Seine, 75004;* **M** *Hôtel de Ville Tel. 01 48 87 74 24 Daily 12 noon–24 pm, Sat., Sun. Brunch 12 noon–16 pm Visa, Master*

Gorgeous setting on Canal St.-Martin. The perfect place to spend a quiet afternoon gazing at the water and having a snack.

Le Petit Gavroche

J 7 *15, rue Ste.-Croix-de-la-Bretonnerie, 75004* **M** *Hôtel de Ville Tel: 01 48 87 74 26 Daily 8 am–11 pm, menu till 10 pm Visa, Master*

Le Petit Gavroche: lunch menu for as little as 45 FF

The lunch menu at this simple little place in the heart of the Marais costs only 45 FF. The good home cooking will satisfy your appetite. And the opportunity to sit among nice, normal people is free of charge.

Antiqui-Thé

K 6 *72, rue Amelot, 75011*
M *St.-Sébastien-Froissard*
Tel: 01 49 29 95 75
Daily 10:30 am–7:30 pm,
later with reservations
No credit cards

Antiqui-Thé: "A cup of tea and this sofa, please!"

Restaurant, tea salon, and antique store combined. At this unique place, you can buy the chair you're sitting on when you leave. You can also rummage through old records. Good, hearty fare. Approx. 150 FF per person.

Cafés

Aux Deux Magots

GH 7 *6, pl. St.-Germain-des-Prés, 75006*
M *St.-Germain*
Tel: 01 45 48 55 25
Daily 7:30 am–1:30 am
Visa, Master, Amex

Aux Deux Magots has always been the major rival of the Café de Flore. They vie for customers and the one tries to be more Parisian than the other. The terrace is the perfect place to people-watch – though it's full of tourists. Regulars prefer to sit inside. *Café crème* for 25 FF.

Café de Flore

GH 7 *172, bd. St.-Germain, 75006*
M *St.-Germain*
Tel: 01 45 48 55 26
Daily 7 am–1:30 am
Visa, Master, Amex

Tourists sit at ground level: Café de Flore

Paris without the legendary Café de Flore? Inconceivable. Parisians have breakfast on the 1st floor – if for no other reason, because of the discretion. *Café crème* for 28 FF.

Le Sainte-Marthe

L 4 *32, rue Ste.-Marthe, 75010;* M *Belleville or Goncourt; Tel: 01 44 84 36 96*
Tues. through Sat.
11 am–2 am,
Sun. 11 am–11 pm
Visa

A stylish bistro, a surprise in this neighborhood. The story: tapas, nice atmosphere, serene music. The café's situated on a small square somewhat removed from the lively nightlife. Very friendly people. Wine 15–25 FF.

Café Marly

H 6 *93, rue de Rivoli, 75001;* M *Palais Royal*
Tel: 01 49 26 06 60
Daily 8 am–2 am
All credit cards

Café Marly: The peek into the Louvre is free of charge

The Costes brothers' café is located in a side wing of the Louvre. A high-quality establishment, though the atmosphere's a little cold. But the terrific view of the galleries compensates for everything.

Le Pick-Clops

J 7 *16, rue Vieille-du-Temple, 75004;* M *Hôtel de Ville or St.-Paul*
Tel: 01 40 29 02 18
Mon. through Sat.
8 am–2 am,
Sun. 9 am–2 am
No credit cards

Another beer? You can afford one at Pick-Clops

A beer drinkers' paradise in Paris. At 15 FF, the brew's a steal. In comparison, the music and the atmosphere are a little brasher. But the small tables are in a great location in the heart of the Marais.

Late-night

Le Grand Café des Capucines

G 5 *4, bd. des Capucines, 75009;* **M** *Opéra*
Tel: 01 43 12 19 00
Daily round the clock
All credit cards

The name is somewhat deceiving. Coffee and cappuccino are not the main attractions here. But the seafood sure is good. Turn-of-the-century décor. Menu from 178 FF, à la carte approx. 250 FF.

Au Pied de Cochon

I 6 *6, rue Coquillière, 75001;* **M** *Les Halles or Châtelet*
Tel: 01 40 13 77 00
Daily round the clock
All credit cards

When Les Halles still housed markets, this restaurant enjoyed a very good reputation due its fresh fish. The cult days are over, but you can still partake of solid food here at all times of day or night. Menu 250 FF.

La Maison Blanche

J 3 *21, rue de Dunkerque, 75010;* **M** *Gare du Nord*
Tel: 01 48 78 15 92
Daily round the clock
All credit cards

Sauerkraut, mussels with french fries, steaks round the clock. A la carte approx. 140 FF, menu from 68 FF.

Terminus Nord

J 3 *23, rue de Dunkerque, 75010;* **M** *Gare du Nord*
Tel: 01 42 85 05 15
Breakfast
7:30 am–10:30 am,

Terminus Nord: seafood at the train station

Hot meals 11 am–1 am
Master, Visa, Amex

A brasserie dating back to the beginning of the 20th century. Excellent menu. The specialty is seafood. Colorfully mixed clientele, from travelers to media people. Approx. 250 FF per person including wine.

Chartier

At the end of the 19th century, Chartier was a "bouillon," a soup kitchen for the simple people of Montmartre. It has retained its charm. The entrance is in a dark courtyard. The daily specials are particularly good – though a little cafeteria-style. The waiters' grumpiness is legendary. A la carte 80–100 FF.

H 4 *7, rue du Fbg. Montmartre, 75009*
M *Grands Boulevards*
Tel: 01 47 70 86 29
Daily 12 noon–3 pm,
7.30 pm–10 pm; Visa, Master

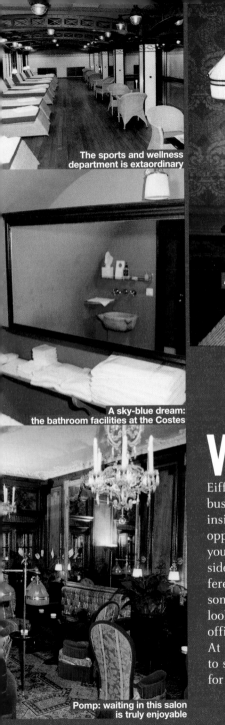

The sports and wellness department is extaordinary

A sky-blue dream: the bathroom facilities at the Costes

Pomp: waiting in this salon is truly enjoyable

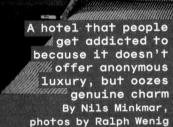

A hotel that people get addicted to because it doesn't offer anonymous luxury, but oozes genuine charm
By Nils Minkmar, photos by Ralph Wenig

While the Ritz has become a normal Parisian attraction like the Eiffel Tower, with full tourist buses outside and empty halls inside, Hotel Costes is just the opposite: an 'in' address that you hardly notice from the outside. Even the reception is different from other hotels: it's somewhat out of the way and looks a little like a notary's office in some country town. At the Costes you don't have to stand while you're waiting for your room key, but you can

Quiet, Luxury and House Music

sit in a plush red chair with a high backrest – without being stared at.

It's no wonder, then, that many people who spend their lives in hotels – the big stars of music, fashion, and art – come to the Costes again and again. They're tired of not knowing which Hilton hotel they've woken up in. The Costes is different. Renovated in the style of a Tuscan villa, and furnished like a house in the novels of Marcel Proust, in different shades of red, with irresistible house music played by the hotel's own DJ every

evening, it's both a meeting place for the Paris scene and at the same time, on the perfectly sound-proof upper floors, a refuge in the sense of Baudelaire's Trias – *calme, luxe et volupte* (quiet, luxury, and sensuality).

On the other hand, strange encounters in the Costes are almost a matter of course. Alice Cooper sticks his reptile-like head out of a door and asks how to get to the ground floor; Donatella Versace rushes down the hallway; Michael Stipe stands at an open window and rehearses new R.E.M. songs.

Hôtel Costes

G 5/6 *239, rue St.-Honoré, 75001*
M *Tuileries; Tel: 01 42 44 50 00,*
Fax 01 42 44 50 01
Prices: single room from 1750 FF,
double room from 2250, suite from 5250 FF
All credit cards

Economy

Tiquetonne Hôtel

16 6, rue Tiquetonne,
75002; **M** *Etienne Marcel*
Tel: 01 42 36 94 58
Fax: 01 42 36 02 94
Closed in August
Prices: single room with
shower and toilet 213 FF,
double room 246 FF,
breakfast 25 FF
Visa, Master

The Tiquetonne is located in a small, quiet side street away from all the hustle and bustle. The rooms aren't very big, but they have showers and toilets.

Hôtel Pratic

J 7 9, rue d'Ormesson,
75004; **M** *St.-Paul*
Tel: 01 48 87 80 47
Fax: 01 48 87 40 04
Prices: single room 290 FF,
double room from 475 FF,
breakfast 45 FF
All credit cards

A friendly hotel not far from the Marais quarter in a quiet little side street. The rooms are simple and clean. If you want more light, avoid the rooms overlooking the courtyard.

Hôtel du Globe

H 8 *15, rue des Quatre-*
Vents, 75006; M *Odéon*
Tel: 01 43 26 35 50
Fax: 01 46 33 62 69
Prices: single room 255 FF,
double room 390–430 FF,
breakfast 45 FF
Visa, Master

A charming hotel in a
16th-century building,
with thick wooden
beams and a brick in-
terior. A special treat:
elegant sofas in the
Louis XV style.

Hôtel St.-Placide

G 8 *6, rue St.-Placide,*
75006; M *Sèvres-Babylone*
or St.-Placide
Tel: 01 45 48 80 08
Fax: 01 45 44 70 32
Prices: single room 280 FF,
double room 380 FF, twin:
460 FF, breakfast 35 FF
Visa, Master

A relatively new hotel
next to the Bon Marché
department store.
Reasonable prices
despite being in an
expensive part of
town. All rooms have
a shower, toilet, mini-
bar, phone, and TV.

Hôtel Picard

JK 6 *26, rue de Picardie,*
75003; M *République or*
Temple; Tel: 01 48 87 53 82
Fax: 01 48 87 02 56
Prices: single room from
210 FF, double room from
250 FF, breakfast 30 FF
Visa, Master

**Hôtel Picard: lavish
breakfasts**

This two-star hotel is
only a stone's throw
from the Place de
la République. The
30 rooms all have a
shower or sink and
a toilet, a phone, and
TV. What's more, eggs
and cheese are served
for breakfast.

Hôtel de Nesle

H 7 *7, rue de Nesle, 75006*
M *Odéon or St.-Germain-*
des-Prés; Tel: 01 43 54 62 41
Prices: single room 275 FF,
double room 350–500 FF
No credit cards

**Hôtel de Nesle: all the
comforts of home**

Undoubtedly one of
the city's most quaint
and homey hotels. The
family-run establish-
ment has 20 rooms,
ten with showers in
the room, ten with
showers in the hall.
The hotel is very quiet.
You have to make
a reservation for
breakfast.

Hôtel de Nice

J 7 *42, rue de Rivoli, 75004*
M *Hôtel de Ville*
Tel: 01 42 78 55 29
Fax: 01 42 78 36 07
Prices: single room 380 FF,
double room 500 FF,
breakfast 35 FF
Visa, Master

Across from the
Hôtel de Ville on a
very lively square.
Family atmosphere
with warm decor. All
rooms have a shower
or bath and a toilet.
The entrance can be
hard to find.

Castex Hôtel

K 8 *5, rue Castex, 75004*
M *Bastille*
Tel: 01 42 72 31 52
Fax: 01 42 72 57 91
Prices: single room with
shower from 250 FF, double
room with shower from
320 FF, breakfast 30 FF
Visa, Master, Amex, Diners

**Castex: affordable
accommodations at
the Bastille**

Small, solid, friendly,
family-run hotel. The
rooms are small but
comfortable. The main
advantages: the reason-
able prices and the
central location at the
Bastille. The front door
is locked after mid-
night, so you need to
know the door code.

Hôtel Bon Séjour

H 2 11, rue Burq, 75018
M *Abbesses or Blanche*
Tel: 01 42 54 22 53
Fax: 01 42 54 25 92
Prices: single room from
120 FF, double room
from 180 FF
No credit cards

Ideal alternative to a youth hostel – somewhat Spartan as some rooms have no shower. Good location in the 18ᵗʰ arrondissement. If you want to paint the 18ᵗʰ red, ask the proprietor, who lives in the building, for a key.

Moderate

Hôtel Chopin

H 4/5 10, bd. Montmartre,
75009; **M** *Grands Boule-*
vards or Richelieu-Drouot
Tel: 01 47 70 58 10
Fax: 01 42 47 00 70
Prices: single room
405–435 FF, double room
450–490 FF, 3 people
565 FF, breakfast 38 FF
Visa, Master, Amex, Diners

Chopin: the name is worthy of a piano

The entrance area with a leather armchair and piano is located in the Jouffroy arcade, built in 1846. The owner has made an effort to

preserve the family-like atmosphere. Nice rooms with new sanitary facilities. Book well in advance!

Hôtel du Panthéon

I 9 19, pl. du Panthéon,
75005; **M** *Luxembourg*
Tel: 01 43 54 32 95
Fax: 01 43 26 64 65
Prices: double room 900 FF,
single room 750 FF,
breakfast 50 FF
Visa, Master, Amex

**Rooms with a view:
Hôtel du Panthéon**

A small, charming hotel. Goes perfectly with the atmosphere of the Jardin du Luxembourg. Ask for one of the rooms on the top floor which command a view all the way to Sacré-Cœur.

Hôtel de la Place du Louvre

H 6 21, rue des Prêtres-
St.-Germain-l'Auxerrois,
75001; **M** *Pont-Neuf or*
Louvre-Rivoli
Tel: 01 42 33 78 68
Fax: 01 42 33 09 95
Prices: single room with
shower 525 FF, single room
with bath 720 FF, double
room/twin with bath
850 FF, breakfast 55 FF
All credit cards

A nice, quaint medieval building with thick, irregular rubble masonry and timber framing. Paying homage to the Louvre

across the way, the rooms are named after famous painters. The breakfast room is housed in an old vault.

Tim Hôtel Montmartre

H 3 11, pl. Emile Goudeau,
75018; **M** *Abbesses*
Tel: 01 42 55 74 79
Fax: 01 42 55 71 01
Prices: double room
from 680 FF, 3 people
room from 810 FF,
breakfast 49 FF
All credit cards

Tim Hôtel: Inspiration for Picasso and Max Ernst

Next to the Bâteau Lavoir, where Picasso and Max Ernst once lived. This is where Picasso painted his famous *Demoiselles d'Avignon*. The beautiful two-star hotel is situated in a splendid location up on the Montmartre hill. Very clean and renovated. From the top floor you have a magnificent view of Paris.

Le Terrasse Hôtel

18ᵉ 12, rue Joseph de
Maistre, 75018; **M** *Clichy*
Tel: 01 46 06 72 85
Fax: 01 42 52 29 11
Prices: apartment 1,770 FF,
double room 1,320 FF,
super double room 1,470 FF,
single room 1,110 to 1,220
FF, small room 890 FF
(all prices include breakfast)
All credit cards

Le Terrasse: breakfast at the foot of Montmartre

The mornings make it especially worthwhile. While breakfasting on the terrace you have a breathtaking panaroma of Paris. The hotel is situated at the foot of Montmartre. All of the rooms are comfortable, some with an *art-deco* touch. The 5th floor is reserved for non-smokers.

Saint Germain

G 7 88, rue du Bac, 75007
M *Rue du Bac*
Tel: 01 49 54 70 00
Fax: 01 45 48 26 89
Prices: double room 750 to 850 FF, breakfast 55 FF
Visa, Master, Amex

Saint Germain: small, flowery, and renovated

This little hotel in St.-Germain has 24 rooms, which are small but have a personal, flowery touch. The

churches and other room rental services

Room rental organizations help you feel at home in Paris

Organisation pour le Tourisme Universitaire (OTU)

I 6 119, rue St.-Martin, 75004; **M** *Les Halles or Rambuteau*
Tel: 01 40 29 12 12
Fax: 01 40 29 12 20
Mon. through Fri.
10 am–6:30 pm,
Sat. 10 am–5 pm

Room rental service and travel organizer for students and young people around the globe. What's more, in the office you can quickly get to know like-minded people from all over the world. It's hard not to when you're waiting in line there at busy times.

Goethe Institute

D 5 17, av. d'Iéna, 75016
M *Iéna*
Tel: 01 44 43 92 30
Fax: 01 44 43 92 40
www.goethe.de/fr
Mon. through Fri.
9 am–9 pm,
library 2 pm–8 pm

Room listings in folders. It's worth

stopping by often as the offer doesn't seem to be updated often, and anything new that comes in goes quickly.

Eglise Allemande

G 3 25, rue Blanche, 75009; **M** *Trinité or Blanche*
Tel: 01 45 26 79 43
Fax: 01 53 20 03 42
Tues. through Fri.
8 am–6 pm

The small church is located close to the St.-Lazare train station. On the bulletin board you can find offers or put up your own.

Eglise Américaine

DE 6 Quai d'Orsay, 75007
M *Pont de l'Alma*

On the Quai d'Orsay, near the cathedral of Les Invalides. The same principle as at the Eglise Allemande. Good place to make contacts.

bathrooms were all renovated recently. Everything is extremely elegant. Ask for a room in the back on the courtyard.

Lenox Montparnasse

G 9 15, rue Delambre, 75014
M *Vavin or Edgar Quinet*
Tel: 01 43 35 34 50
Fax: 01 43 20 46 64
Prices: double room from 560 FF, suite from 1050 FF, breakfast 50 FF
All credit cards

Lenox: fashion designers need peace and quiet too

Small, pleasant, friendly hotel near the Boulevard Montparnasse, around the corner from La Coupole. The *art-deco* bar is striking. During prêt-à-porter shows, the fashion scene hangs out here and recovers from all the stress.

Le Clos Médicis

H 8 56, rue Monsieur-le-Prince, 75006; **M** *Odéon*
Tel: 01 43 29 10 80
Fax: 01 43 54 26 90
Double room 790–1,200 FF
All credit cards

You don't need to make a side-trip to Provence, because the atmosphere and decorations here are very Provençal. The building was erected in 1860 and has a very charming courtyard. We recommend taking a room with a balcony, though it costs 1,090 FF.

Le Clos Médicis: more than a touch of Provence

Le Sheraton (Paris Airport Hôtel)

Roissy Aérogare 2, Charles de Gaulles, BP 30051, 95716 Roissy Aérogare, **M** *RER Charles de Gaulle, Aéroport 2*
Tel: 01 48 62 36 56
Fax: 01 49 19 70 71
Prices: conventional room 2,050 FF, club 2,250 FF,
"smart" room 2,900 FF, breakfast 135 FF, during trade shows + 500 FF
Visa, Master, Amex, Diners

This hotel, located in the middle of the airport, opened in February 1996. It looks like a mega-steamer. The smooth stone and window façade on the exterior is not very inviting. But interior designer Andrée Putman created rooms flooded with light. A practical aspect: you have direct access to Terminal 2 and the new TGV rail station.

Lancaster

E 4 7, rue de Berri (at the Champs-Elysées), 75008
M *Franklin Roosevelt*
Tel: 01 40 76 40 76
Fax: 01 40 76 40 00
Prices: single room from 1,650 FF, double room from 2,350 FF, breakfast 120 FF
Visa, Master, Amex, Diners

In the 20s and 30s a hotel for the stars. Marlene Dietrich, Orson Welles, and Cary Grant slept here

Necessary Numbers

If you're planning to visit someone at home in Paris, you need a good memory for numbers

If you meet Monsieur or Mademoiselle Right, and after talking for hours in a bar you get their address, it doesn't mean a thing if they don't give you a short, secret number: the door code. Without one people don't have anything in Paris:

no home, no friends, no work. Because all doors are locked; it's as though the city were in a state of siege, and only when you type in the right combination on the silver keys next to the entrance will the drawbridge go down.

when they were working in Paris. Since 1996, Grace Léo-Andrieu has imbued it with elegance once again. The 60 large rooms are full of antiques and artworks, yet still *tour de forces* of design.

Luxury

Le Lutétia

G 8 *45, bd. Raspail, 75006*
M *Sèvres-Babylone*
Tel: 01 49 54 46 46
Fax: 01 49 54 46 00
*Prices: "supérior" room
1,800 FF, suite from 4,500
FF, breakfast 75 to 145 FF
Visa, Master, Amex, Diners*

**A feast for the eyes:
La Lutetia**

The individual suites are as large as four-room apartments, but then again, you can pay the equivalent of a month's rent for just one night. Those who can afford to stay here will love the cosy lounge and the Brasserie Lutétia, which boasts divine seafood. And those who can't can at least admire

the glamorous hotel, which is illuminated at night, from the outside.

Le Pavillon de la Reine

K 7 *28, pl. des Vosges,
75003;* **M** *St.-Paul or Bastille*
Tel: 01 40 29 19 19
Fax: 01 40 29 19 20
*Prices: rooms from 1,700 FF,
junior suite from 2,350 FF
Visa, Master, Amex, Diners*

**Le Pavillon: charming
and luxurious courtyard**

The address is deceiving. The hotel is not on Place des Vosges, but located behind the row of buildings. You walk through an archway and across a – pretty courtyard. But the fact that there are no rooms with views of the square does not detract from the experience one bit. The hotel is simply gorgeous, luxurious yet still cozy. And the location's out of this world – in the heart of the Marais close to the Bastille.

Le Westminster

G 5 *13, rue de la Paix,
75002;* **M** *Opéra*
Tel: 01 42 61 57 46
Fax: 01 42 60 30 66
*Prices: standard from
2,400 FF, junior suite
4,400 FF, breakfast 150 FF
All credit cards*

**A lobby with character:
Le Westminster**

The rooms of this 150-year-old hotel have all been renovated in the last two years. But luckily, the building hasn't lost any of its charm. The rooms with marble fireplaces are especially stunning. Another plus: the location between the Tuileries and the Ritz.

Le Raphael

CD 4 *17, av. Kléber, 75017*
M *Kléber*
Tel: 01 53 64 32 00
Fax: 01 53 64 32 01
*Prices: rooms from
2,340 FF, junior suite
3,720 FF, room with
balcony 10,000 FF,
breakfast from 135 FF
Visa, Master, Amex, Diners*

This hotel, which opened in 1925, is somewhat removed from the bustle of the city. It's located on one of the streets forming a star at the Place Etoile, the site of the Arc de Triomphe. The Champs-Elysées starts here, so hotel guests can stroll and shop nearby. Very elegant atmosphere. The site is often used as a film location and a photo motif. The rooms with balconies command a fine view of the Eiffel Tower.

Historic island location: Henri IV

Pensions

Pension Cardinal

G 3 *4, rue Cardinal Mercier, 75009;* **M** *Liège*
Tel + Fax: 01 48 74 16 16
Prices: single room 210 FF, double room 238–280 FF
No credit cards

A quiet place where you feel at home at once, if only because it's very tidy and clean. Rooms with and without showers. The rooms are bright, some even with balconies. The courtyard is very pretty. No hot food is served in the hotel, but you can buy your own eats and put them in the fridge.

Henri IV

H 7 *25, pl. Dauphine, 75001;* **M** *Pont-Neuf*
Tel: 01 43 54 445 3
Prices (including breakfast): single room with sink 120 FF, double room with shower 285 FF
No credit cards

This small *pension* is located on the Île de la Cité on the charming Place Dauphine in a 400-year-old building. Breakfast with a view of the tree-lined square. Simple comfort and low prices.

Les Sans-Culottes

K 7 *27, rue de Lappe, 75011;* **M** *Bastille*
Tel: 01 49 23 85 80
Fax: 01 48 05 08 56
Prices including breakfast: double room 350 FF, single room 300 FF
Visa, Master, Amex, Diners

Small, charming pension covered with ivy. There are only ten rooms. Perfect place to access the rue de Lappe, which comes alive at night. A wrought-iron *art nouveau* staircase leads to the hotel's upper floors.

Au Palais Gourmand

G 9 *120, bd. Raspail, 75006*
M *Notre-Dame-des-Champs*
Tel: 01 45 48 24 15
Fax: 01 42 22 33 41
Prices: single room 180–394 FF, double room 397–474 FF
No credit cards

A pension with a family atmosphere. Everyone eats together. And the whole show is run by the *pension* mama, from whom you can get drinks and sandwiches when you're hungry – in exchange for francs, of course. This *pension* opened back in 1920.

Apartments

Citadines Apparthotels

F 9 *67, av. du Maine, 75006*
M *Montparnasse-Bienvenue or Gaîté*
Tel: 01 41 05 79 79
Fax: 01 47 59 04 70
www.citadines.com
Prices: studette (1 person.) 545 FF, studio (2 people) 650 FF, 1,250 FF
Visa, Master, Amex, Diners

Not far from the Jardin du Luxembourg. Functionally furnished apartments which can be rented for a night, a week, or a month, with bathroom, kitchen, and TV.

Paris Appartements

H 5 *69, rue d'Argout, 75002*
M *Sentier*
Tel: 01 40 28 01 28
Fax: 01 40 28 92 01
Prices: 2-room apartment around 800 FF per day
Visa, Master, Amex

If you're in Paris on business and the company's picking up the tab, you can stay here in centrally located furnished apartments.

Youth hostels

Young and happy

I 9 *8o, rue Mouffetard,
75005;* M *Place Monge
Tel: 01 45 35 09 53
Fax: 01 47 07 22 24
Prices (including breakfast):
dormitory-stily room107 FF,
double room 127 FF
No credit cards*

**Young and happy: a tip
for party animals**
A typical youth hostel:
showers and toilets in
the hall, only a few
rooms with showers.

The advantage: the
location on the Rue
Mouffetard, ideal for
going out, no cars.
The hostel closes at 2
in the morning; recep-
tion open around the
clock.

Auberge Internationale des Jeunes

L 8 *10, rue Trousseau,
75011,* M *Ledru-Rollin
Tel: 01 47 00 62 00
Fax: 01 47 00 33 16
Prices (including breakfast):
91 FF; open 24 hours,
rooms closed from
10 am–3 pm
Visa, Master, Amex*

Cheap, friendly, attrac-
tive youth hostel not
far from the Bastille
quarter. A plus: the
lavish breakfast.

Le Jules Ferry

K 5 *8, bd. Jules Ferry, 75011*
M *République
Tel: 01 43 57 55 60
Fax: 01 40 21 79 92
Prices (including breakfast):
dormitory-style room 115 FF,
double room 120 FF
Visa, Master*

**Ferry: a youth hostel
with principles**
An official youth
hostel requiring
written registration
and a youth hostel
ID. The latter can be
bought on the premis-
es. Nightowls take
heed: rooms have to
be vacated by 2 pm.

Camping in the Metropolis

**The Bois de Boulogne is one of Europe's most
beautiful city parks. Camping fans can enjoy
nature a stone's throw from the big city**

It's near the city yet in the middle of the woods. A great
combination in Paris. On the western edge of the Bois de
Boulogne you can put up your tent on a beautiful site, and
you don't even have to make reservation. If you're traveling
by car, take the N 185 to the Bois de Bologne, and you'll
see a sign. From the campground you're not only close to
the city, but also to beautiful natural surroundings. You can
take romantic bike or boat trips in the forest, or simply
relax in the fresh air. A shuttle bus travels back and forth
between the Métro station and the campground.

16e *Allée du Bord de l'Eau, 75016*
M *Pte Maillot; Tel: 01 45 24 30 00, Fax: 01 42 24 42 95
Open 8:30 am–1 pm; Prices: 140–220 FF; Amex, Master, Visa, Diners*

A Night in

Art has to be well guarded. Even at night. That's the job of museum night watchmen. But what do they do all night long? "Sleep!" say Alain Sonneville and Pierre-Claude de Castro. And they say that sleeping in museums is an art

By Kia Vahland

When Alain Sonneville goes to a museum, he'd just as soon fall asleep. For the museum, that's great praise. After all, he doesn't sleep everywhere. Only next to precious originals. Other people have copies or reproductions hanging above their beds, and are surprised when they don't sleep well. Alain Sonneville knows that to sleep really soundly you need the real thing.

However, the artist can't afford a Raphael or a Rodin for his bedroom. But he has a job at which he can sleep next to masterpieces. He's a night watchman at the Musée Rodin. So everything is where it belongs: the works of art in public view, and Alain's bed near the works of art.

Alain has a friend at the Musee Guimet named Pierre Claude de Castro. The two are inseparable – except in bed. Their cots are so small only one person can sleep in them. But the professional sleepers aren't alone; usually there's a beautiful woman nearby. "I dream best when I sleep below the dancing Khmer goddess from the 10th century," enthuses Pierre-Claude. She lulls him so well, he says, that if it weren't for the red alarm clock at her feet he would sleep past the time when the museum opens.

The sleep artist Alain, too, chooses his place of rest carefully.

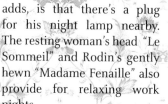

He prefers to put up his cot next to Rodin's famous sculpture "The Kiss." "I have erotic dreams," he says, rolling his eyes suggestively. Another advantage of "The Kiss," he adds, is that there's a plug for his night lamp nearby. The resting woman's head "Le Sommeil" and Rodin's gently hewn "Madame Fenaille" also provide for relaxing work nights.

Sometimes the night watchman dreams that he opens the museum doors for a delivery man and he covers the floor with vegetables. Fortunately, no one really enters the museum at night. Alain, his fellow watchman, and the sculptures are left in peace.

After the museums close, they can make themselves at home. Aside from an occasional round to make sure everything's okay, there's not much to do. "Perfect for lazy people like us," say the two artists.

Museums

Le Louvre

H 6 *33–36, quai du Louvre 75001;* **M** *Musée du Louvre Tel: 01 40 20 51 51 Wed. through Mon. 9 am–6 pm, Mon., Wed. open till 9:45 pm www.louvre.fr Price: 45 FF; reduced prices starting at 3 pm, Sun. 26 FF Free admission: the first Sunday of every month for everyone under 18 as well as school groups and the unemployed Advance booking: Tel: 01 49 87 54 54*

The first thing to buy is a weekly schedule providing information on special exhibitions in the Louvre and all adjoining rooms. Because the world's largest museum, which has over 56,000 square yards of exhibition space, houses an incredible number of masterpieces. Set aside a lot of time.

The Louvre: you could spend a lifetime there

Jeu de Paume

F 5 1, *pl. de la Concorde,*
75001; M *Concorde*
Tel: 01 47 03 12 50
Tues. 12 noon–9:30 pm,
Wed. through Fri.
12 noon– 7 pm,
Sat., Sun. 10 am–7 pm
Price: 38 FF, reduced 28 FF

Changing exhibitions
of contemporary art.

Musée Picasso

K 6 *Hôtel Salé, 5, rue de*
Thorigny, 75003
M *St.-Paul*
Tel: 01 42 71 25 21
Wed. through Mon.
in summer 9:30 am–6 pm,
in winter 9:30 am–5:30 pm
Admission: 30 FF,
reduced 20 FF

This former city
palace, which boasts
magnificient architec-
ture and was built
for a salt tax collector
in the 17ᵗʰ century,
houses an extensive
collection of paintings
and sculptures by
Pablo Picasso.

**Musée Picasso: the
master beckons**

Maison de Victor Hugo

K 7 *Hôtel de Rohan-Gué-*
menée, 6, pl. des Vosges,
75004; M *Bastille or Chemin*
Vert; Tel: 01 42 72 10 16

Tues. through Sun.
10 am–5:40 pm
Admission: 22 FF, free for
people 27 and under

Documentation of the
life and work of the
famous French writer.
Victor Hugo lived here
from 1832 to 1848
before being exiled
to the channel island
Jersey.

**Victor Hugo: last stop
before exile**

Centre Pompidou

I 6 *Pl. Beaubourg, 75004*
M *Rambuteau or Les Halles*
Tel: 01 44 78 12 33
Mon., Fri. 12 noon–10 pm,
Sat., Sun. 10 am–10 pm

Futuristic steel-and-
glass art and culture
temple. Though highly
controversial when it
was built, today it's
one of Paris' main at-
tractions. It's been
closed for renovations
since September 1997,
scheduled to reopen at
the turn-of-the-millen-
nium. Apart from the
museum of modern
art, it houses a library,
a *cinémathèque,* a cen-
ter for commercial de-
sign, and an institute
for acoustics and
music.

**Pompidou: art for the
third millennium**

Musée Carnavalet

J 7 *Hôtel Carnavalet,*
23, rue de Sévigné, 75003
M *St.-Paul*
Tel: 01 42 72 21 13
Tues. through Sun.
10 am–17:40 pm
Admission: 35 FF,
reduced 25 FF

City history mueum:
paintings, drawings,
and engravings with
views of Paris and
historic scenes; recon-
structed rooms such
as Marcel Proust's
bedroom.

**Carnavalet: a peek at
historic bedrooms**

Musée National d'Histoire Naturelle

J 9 *Jardin des plantes, 36,*
rue Geoffroy-St.-Hilaire,
75005; M *Austerlitz or*
Jussieu
Tel: 01 40 79 30 00
Evolution gallery: Wed.
through Sun. 10 am–6 pm,
Thurs. till 10 pm

*Admission: 40 FF, reduced
30 FF, tours: Sat. 2:30 pm,
30 FF; Mineralogy, Paleon-
tology and Comparative
Anatomy galleries: Wed.
through Sun. 10 am–5 pm
Admission: 30 FF, reduced,
20 FF; Tropical greenhouses:
Wed. through Sun. 1 pm–
5 pm, 15 FF, reduced rate
10 FF; Ménagerie:
Tel: 01 40 79 37 94; daily
9 am–5 pm; admission:
30 FF, reduced rate 20 FF;
Microzoo: free with
admission ticket for the
Ménagerie (11 and above)*

The museum is locat-
ed at the entrance to
the Jardin des Plantes.
In the park: 19th-cen-
tury glass and iron
greenhouses, a palm
garden, a labyrinth,
a small *ménagerie*,
and a zoo. It was here
that Rainer Maria
Rilke was inspired
to write the poem
"The Panther."

Musée Maillol-
Fondation Dina
Vierny

*F 7 59-61, rue de Grenelle
75007; M Rue du Bac
Tel: 01 42 22 59 58
Wed. through Mon.
11 am–6 pm
Admission: 40 FF,
reduced rate 26 FF,
free for people 18 and
under*

Vierny: classical out-
side, modern art inside

Situated in the heart
of St.-Germain, this
small museum stages
first-class exhibitions
of contemporary art.

Palais de la
Découverte

*E 5 Av. Franklin-D. Roosevelt,
75008; M Franklin Roose-
velt; Tel: 01 40 74 80 00
Group tours:
Tel: 01 40 74 80 15
Tues. through Sat.
9:30 am–6 pm,
Sun. 10 am–7 pm
Admission: 30 FF, reduced
rate 20 FF, free for children
5 and under, 13 FF more
for the planetarium*

Science made fun.
All kinds of interest-
ing experiments are
shown. The planetari-
um is state of the art.

Musée de
l'Erotisme

*H 3 72, bd. de Clichy, 75018
M Blanche
Tel: 01 42 58 28 73
www.erotic-museum.com*

*Daily 10 am–2 pm
Admission: 40 FF,
reduced rate 30 FF*

The collection in-
cludes over 2,000
sculptures and paint-
ings from Asia, Latin
America, Europe, and
Oceania.

Musée Grévin

*H 4/5 10, bd. Montmartre,
75009; M Grands Boule-
vards
Tel: 01 47 70 87 99
Daily 1 pm–7 pm
Admission: 58 FF,
reduced rate 38 FF*

Grévin: waxing historical

A budding art scene

Right next to Chinatown, a new avant-garde
gallery district is emerging. Six young gallerists
have opened galleries on the rue Louise Weiss.
The area is starting to liven up. The energy of
the art scene springing up here is palpable.

Paris' waxworks with around 5,000 people from yesterday and today.

Musée Edith Piaf

L 5 *5–7, rue Crespin du Gast, 75011*
M *Ménilmontant*
Tel: 01 43 55 52 72
Admission: 10 FF

Tiny museum in the private apartment of the world-famous *chanson* singer from Belleville. You have to make an appointment by phone to visit the museum.

Musée National des Arts d'Afrique et d'Océanie

M 9 *293, av. Daumesnil, 75012;* M *Pte Dorée*
Tel: 01 44 74 84 80
Wed. through Mon. 10 am–5:30 pm
Admission: 30 FF, reduced 20 FF, exhibitions 38 FF, reduced rate 28 FF

This temple-like museum is situated in a splendid park. African and Oceanic art is on show. There's a tropical aquarium in the basement.

Out of Africa: art in the Musée National

Musée Bourdelle

F 9 *16, rue Antoine Bourdelle, 75015;* M *Montparnasse-Bienvenue or Falguière*
Tel: 01 49 54 73 73
Tues. through Sun. 10 am–17:40 pm; admission: 17 FF, reduced rate 9.50 FF, exhibition + museum 27 FF, reduced rate 19 FF

Today the sculptor's former studio is used to exhibit his huge works, as well as paintings and drawings. Interesting garden.

Bourdelle: formerly a studio, today a museum

Fondation Le Corbusier

A 7 *Villa la Roche, 55, rue Docteur Blanche, 75016*
M *Jasmin; Mon. through Fri. 10 am–12:30 pm, 1:30 pm–6 pm*

Gallery Branches

K 10/11 *75013;* M *Chevaleret*

Art: Concept

34, rue Louise Weiss
Tel: 01 43 60 90 30
Fax: 01 53 50 90 31
Tues. through Fri. 2 pm–7 pm, Sat. 11 am–7 pm

Air de Paris

34, rue Louise Weiss
Tel: 01 44 23 02 77
Fax 01 53 61 22 84
Tues. through Sat. 2 pm–7 pm

Galerie Emanuel Perrotin

30, rue Louise Weiss
Tel: 01 42 16 79 79
Fax 01 42 16 79 74
Tues. through Fri. 2 pm–7 pm, Sat. 11 am–7 pm

Galerie Praz-Delavallade

28, rue Louise Weiss
Tel: 01 45 86 20 00
Fax 01 45 86 20 10
Tues. through Sat. 11 am–7 pm

Galerie Almine Rech

24, rue Louise Weiss
Tel: 01 45 86 20 00
Fax 01 45 86 20 10
Tues. through Sat. 11 am–7 pm

Jennifer Flay

20, rue Louise Weiss
Tel: 01 42 16 79 79
Fax 01 42 16 79 74
Tues. through Fri. 2 pm–7 pm, Sat. 11 am–7 pm

Villa built in 1923 by Le Corbusier with drawings and blueprints by the architect and a library. Tucked away at the end of a small private street in a nice, quiet quarter.

Le Corbusier: the godfather of design

Sunday Dinner

When Jim Haynes, born in the United States and now residing in Paris, has people over for dinner, he asks his guests to "talk, talk, talk!" To be chez Jim means to spend an evening in a magnificent old salon. To indulge in delicious food, choice wines, and to talk, talk, talk. With all kinds of people ranging from bus drivers and diplomats to DJs and exchange students. Anyone who likes to chat can be put on the guest list of the author, media teacher, and co-founder of the London Art Lab. All you have to do is call a few days in advance. "What's your name, what do you do?" Haynes will ask. Then he'll say: "Good, I'm looking forward to seeing you, darling!" – and you've been officially invited to have dinner in his courtyard domicile. Around 30 people meet on Sundays at 8 pm in the middle of the 14th arrondissement. "You just have to be open and want to meet other people," says Haynes. It's a conversational trip around the world, moving from the open kitchen to the studio bathed in sunlight. People speak French and English – but never sitting down. Because, Haynes says, "When you're standing, you change your conversation partner more often."
Contact: Jim_Haynes@wanadoo.fr
Tel: 01 43 27 17 67

Musée de la Mode de la Ville de Paris

D 5 10, av. Pierre-1er de Serbie, 75016; **M** Iéna
Tel: 01 47 20 85 23
Tues. through Sun.
10 am–6 pm
Admission: 45 FF, 32 FF
Whether it's Givenchy, Dior or Louis XIV – here you can find the most precious attire from many art epochs in the former palace of Graf Galliera. A small, temple-like building housing opulent fashion treasures.

R&L Beaubourg

I 7 23, rue du Renard, 75004; **M** Hôtel de Ville
Tel: 01 44 59 27 27
Tues. through Sat. 10:30 am –1 pm, 2:30 pm–7 pm, closed in August
This 'in' gallery shows works by modern and contemporary artistis, including Andy Warhol, Frank Stella, and Calvin Klein.

Karsten Greve

K 6 *5, rue Debelleyme,
75003;* **M** *St.-Sébastien-
Froissart; Tel: 01 42 77 19 37
Tues. through Sat.
11 am–7 pm*

The prominent
Cologne gallerist
has a branch in the
Marais. On offer:
Twombly, Fontana,
Prangenberg.

**Karsten Greve:
greetings from Cologne**

Thaddaeus Ropac

K 6 *7, rue Debelleyme,
75003;* **M** *St.-Sébastien-
Froissart; Tel: 01 42 72 99 00
Tues. through Sat.
10 am–7 pm*

Right next to the
Karsten Greve gallery.
Contemporary and
avant-garde art on two
floors in an elaborately
renovated building.

Centre Culturel Suisse

J 7 *38, rue Francs-
Bourgeois, 75003*
M *St.-Paul
Tel: 01 42 71 44 50
Wed. through Sat.
2 pm–7 pm*

A futuristic artistic
pearl in the Marais.
Mainly presents video
installations, paint-
ings, and art photog-
raphy.

Louise Leiris

EF 3 *47, rue de Monceau,
75008;* **M** *Monceau
Tel: 01 45 63 20 56;
Tues. through Sat.
10 am–12 noon,
2:30 pm–6 pm*

The monumental
building houses an
elegant, museum-like
gallery with classical
modern works. It's lo-
cated behind Monceau
Park. The collection
of the Picasso dealer
D. H. Kahnweiler is
managed here.

Galerie Le Sous-sol

L 7 *9, rue de Charonne,
75011;* **M** *Bastille
Tel: 01 47 00 02 75
Tues. through Sat.
2:30 pm–7 pm*

There's no sign at the
gallery's entrance, so
keep your eyes peeled.
An archway leads to a
concealed, pretty court-
yard harboring a young,
active gallery with
modern interior which
stages exhibitions of
the works of young
artists.

Galerie 213

G 10 *213, bd. Raspail,
75014;* **M** *Vavin
Tel: 01 43 22 83 23
Tues. through Sat.
11 am–7 pm*

Marion de Beaupré,
formerly an agent for
fashion photographers
such as Peter Lindbergh
and Thierry Le Goues,
opened this gallery two
years ago. A place
where even lesser-
known artists can find access
to a large audience.

Plus: it has a very nice,
well-stocked photo
library.

**213: the library alone
merits a visit**

Robert Capia

HI 6 *24–26, Galerie
Véro-Dodat, 75001*
M *Palais Royal
Tel: 01 42 36 25 94
Mon. through Sat.
10 am–7 pm*

Small, quaint gallery
in the old Véro-Dodat
arcade specializing in
loving restauration
of old dolls.

Agathe Gaillard

J 7 *3, rue du Pont Louis-
Philippe, 75004*
M *Pont-Marie
Tel: 01 42 77 38 24
Tues. through Sat.
1 pm–7 pm, closed in sum-
mer till September 1st*

One of Paris' oldest
photo galleries, with
classic works by such
artists as Lartigue,
Cartier-Bresson, and
Gisèle Freund. Leafing
through the countless
folders is quite fasci-
nating.

**Agathe Gaillard: like in
the good old days**

Opera

Opéra Bastille

K 8 *Pl. de la Bastille
130, rue de Lyon, 75012*
M *Bastille*
*Tel: 0140 01 19 70
Tours: 50 FF
Reservations:
Tel: 08 36 69 78 68
Admission: opera 60–
670 FF, ballet 30–355 FF,
concerts 45–255 FF.
Amex, Diners, Master, Visa*

**Bastille: a young opera
with young artists**

The modern opera
house in Paris is still
being criticized today,
nearly ten years after
its opening. Built to
commemorate the 200th
anniversary of the
French Revolution, the
house is still suffering
from scandal. The pro-
gram is worth seeing
thanks to the young,
committed directors
and performers.

Opéra Comique

H 5 *Pl. Boïeldieu, 75002*
M *Richelieu-Drouot*
*Tel: 01 42 44 45 46
Admission: 50–500 FF
Amex, Diners, Master,
Visa*

Many classics in the
history of opera were
premiered here, "Car-
men" among them.

Even today the comic
opera is a terrific ad-
dress for somewhat
more modest-scaled
operas and unusual
productions.

Palais Garnier

G 4 *Pl. de l'Opéra, 75009*
M *Opéra; Tel: 01 40 01 18 58
Reservations:
Tel: 08 36 69 78 68
Admission: opera 60–670 FF,
ballett 30–355 FF,
concerts 45–255 FF
The house is closed from
July 15 to September
Amex, Diners, Master, Visa*

There are more reasons
than the music to
attend this opera. For
instance, the gigantic
ceiling fresco by Marc
Chagall with famous
opera motifs. Or the
magnificent foyer.
Charles Garnier built
the edifice in 1875.

**Garnier: one of the stars
is named Chagall**

Theater

Théâtre les Déchargeurs

I 7 *3, rue des Déchargeurs,
75001;* M *Châtelet
Tel: 01 42 36 00 02
Admission: cabaret 60–
120 FF, theater 90–120 FF
No credit cards*

In a tiny auditorium
with red velvet chairs,
mainly contemporary

and modern plays are
staged, in the cellar
primarily cabaret. After
the performance, you
can sit together with
the artists at the bar.

**Déchargeurs: here's
to you and you with a
stage star**

culture

Théâtre Lucernaire

G 9 53, rue Notre-Dame des Champs, 75006
M Vavin or Notre-Dame-des-Champs
Tel: 01 45 44 57 34
Advance booking: Mon. through Sat. 2 pm–9 pm
Reservations Mon. through Fri. 10 am–12:30 pm
Admission: 140/120 FF, reduced 90/75 FF
Master

Saint Exupéry's *Little Prince* has told the story of love and friendship here for 20 years now. In the pleasant ambience of the art center, movies are also shown in three cinemas.

Comédie Française

H 6 Salle Richelieu, Pl. Colette, 75001; M Palais-Royal
Tel: 01 44 58 14 00
Admission: 30 FF to 190 FF
Reservations:
Tel: 01 44 58 15 15
Daily 11 am–18 pm
Amex, Visa, Master

Comédie Française: even today the classics are cherished

National theater at the Palais Royal. In the repertory: classics by Molière, Marivaux, and Nerval.

Théâtre Grévin

H 4/5 10, bd. Montmartre, 75009; M Grands Boulevards
Tel: 01 42 46 84 74 and 01 49 87 53 53
Advance booking: Tues. through Sat. 3:30 pm–7:30 pm, Mon. 3 pm–7 pm
Admission: 160 FF, reduced 100 FF
No credit cards

Every afternoon there are shows by magicians, jugglers, and pantomimes –

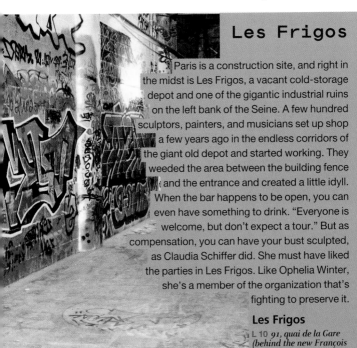

Les Frigos

Paris is a construction site, and right in the midst is Les Frigos, a vacant cold-storage depot and one of the gigantic industrial ruins on the left bank of the Seine. A few hundred sculptors, painters, and musicians set up shop a few years ago in the endless corridors of the giant old depot and started working. They weeded the area between the building fence and the entrance and created a little idyll. When the bar happens to be open, you can even have something to drink. "Everyone is welcome, but don't expect a tour." But as compensation, you can have your bust sculpted, as Claudia Schiffer did. She must have liked the parties in Les Frigos. Like Ophelia Winter, she's a member of the organization that's fighting to preserve it.

Les Frigos

L 10 91, quai de la Gare (behind the new François Mitterand library), 75013
Tel: 01 44 24 96 96

and they don't only appeal to children. And since 1984 classical music concerts have been held in the historic theater auditorium on Sunday mornings and Monday evenings.

Bouffes du Nord

JK 3 *37bis, bd. de la Cha-pelle, 75010;* M *La Chapelle Advance booking: Tel: 01 46 07 34 50 Mon. through Sat. 10 am–6 pm; admission: 70–150 FF; Visa*

Rather dilapidated Belle-Époque theater where Peter Brook staged the nine-hour Indian epic "Mahab-harata" with a multi-national ensemble. Otherwise a mixture of classical and modern plays.

Bouffes du Nord: soft seats for nine hours

Dance

Centre de Danse du Marais

J 6 *41, rue du Temple, 75004;* M *Hôtel de Ville Tel: 01 42 72 15 42 www.cogitel-forum.fr/marais Daily 9 am–10:30 pm Price: 40 FF annual contri-bution + course costs, 90 FF an hour; no credit cards*

A dance school with a diverse offer rang-ing from ballet to jazz, hip hop, tango, and salsa all the way to yoga. For beginners and advanced.

Centre de Danse: dancing up a storm

Ménagerie de Verre

L 6 *12, rue Léchevin, 75011,* M *Parmentier Tel: 01 43 38 33 44 Opening hours: 9 am–7 pm www.multimania.com/ menagerie*

The Ménagerie de verre opened in 1983 and focuses on con-temporary dance, theater, and film. Famous dance people have worked here, including Pina Bausch and Patrick Dupond, Nat Finkelstein and Philippe Découfle.

Movie Theaters

Gaumont Grand Ecran Italie

J 11 *30, pl. d'Italie, 75013* M *Place d'Italie Tel: 08 36 68 75 13 (infor-mation), 01 40 30 30 31 (reservations) Admission: 45–48 FF Visa*

A complex with seven theaters. The Salle Prestige has a giant screen with THX. The cinemas show current movies, usually French versions.

Le Grand Rex

I 5 *1, bd. Poissonnière, 75002;* M *Bonne-Nouvelle Tel: 08 36 68 05 96 Admission: 50 FF, Mondays 40 FF; Visa*

When it opened in 1932, it was celebrat-ed as Europe's largest movie theater. A huge auditorium with 2,800 seats and baroque décor. The program consists of block-busters in French-language versions.

Max Linder Panorama

I 5 *24, bd. Poissonnière, 75009;* M *Grands Boule-vards; Tel: 01 48 24 88 88 (information), 01 40 30 30 31 (reserva-tions); admission: 49 FF, Mon., Wed. 38 FF Visa*

The best sound in Paris. THX par excel-lence – in a large, very comfortable audi-torium with a giant screen and original versions with French subtitles.

MK2 Quai de la Seine

L 2 *14, quai de la Seine, 75019;* M *Stalingrad or Jaurès Tel: 08 36 68 14 07 (infor-mation), 01 40 30 30 31 (reservations) Admission: 50 FF; Visa*

The six auditoriums aren't huge, but they're big enough for comfortable viewing. A short film is shown before every main attraction. The café adjacent is the perfect place for a rendezvous before the show.

MK2: a short film is included in the price

Studio Galande

I 8 *42, rue Galande, 75005*
M *St.-Michel*
Tel: 01 43 26 94 08,
01 43 54 72 71
(information)
Admission: 44 FF,
Wednesdays 34 FF
No credit cards

An institution. For years now the "Rocky Horror Picture Show" has been screened on Fridays at 10:30 pm and Saturdays at 12:30 am. Good repertory cinema.

Libraries

Forney

J 7 *1, rue du Figuier, 75004*
M *Pont-Marie or St.-Paul*
Tel: 01 42 78 14 60
Tues. through Fri.
1:30 pm–8:30 pm,
Sat. 10 am–8:30 pm

The comprehensive art and technology library is housed in the Hôtel de Sens,

considered one of Paris' finest palaces. Up to six books can be checked out per person per day.

Forney: technological literature, straight from a palace

Bibliothèque du Film

L 8 *100, rue du Fbg. St.-Antoine, 75012*
M *Ledru-Rollin*
Tel: 01 53 02 22 40
Archives: Mon. through Fri. 10 am–7 pm; iconothèque: Mon. through Fri. 10 am– 1 pm, 2 pm–5:30 pm

Offers deep insight into the world of cinema. This highly modern library houses approx. 35,000 documents about cinema, among other things, 13,000 books and newspapers as well as original placards and 1,100 films.

Bibliothèque Nationale de France François Mitterand

L 10/11 *11, quai François Mauriac, 75013*
M *Quai de la Gare*
Tel: 01 53 79 59 59
Tues. through Sat. 10 am– 8 pm, Sun. 12 noon–7 pm
www.bnf.fr
Fee: 20 FF per day, yearly pass 200 FF

The new national library, designed by Dominique Perrault in the shape of four open books, is a literary temple. The building, whose exterior consists solely of steel and glass and which has imposing towers of books, is not just a must for architecture lovers. It's already become a Paris landmark.

Roger-Viollet Agence Photographique

H 7 *6, rue de Seine, 75006*
M *Odéon or St.-Germain- des-Prés; Tel: 01 55 42 89 00*
www.roger-viollet.fr
Mon. through Fri. 9 am–6 pm

The world's most important collection of photos – more than seven million documents. In 1937 the daughter of the photographer Henri Roger-Viollet, Hélène, and her husband Jean Fischer, bought the little place and founded the renowned *Documentation Générale Photographique.*

Roger-Viollet: a true photo encyclopedia

They call themselves Yamakasi, and what they do is crazy. They climb around on highrise buildings, without nets or other equipment. They climb as though it were a life or death matter. And that's just what it is

A Leap into

By Astrid Mayer, photos by Ralph Mecke

They're always performing death-defying feats – no wonder passers-by think they're totally nuts. But nothing has ever happened

The nicer buildings in Evry are made of brick – the cathedral, for instance, which looks like a giant cake with a visor, or the town hall. "Brick's no good for climbing," says Yann, "concrete is better." And there's more than enough concrete in Evry. Evry is one of those Parisian suburbs which concrete manufacturers still apologize for as an example of how not to build using their raw material.

Face to face with the precipice:
With the instinct of sleepwalkers,
the Yamakasis make death-defying
leaps – for a better life

Too late for Yann and his gang. They have to make do. Yann's doctors says that what he does everyday is destroying his joints, that one day he could break his neck. Still, the Yamakasis feel they must persist. Otherwise they'll never get out of the miserable suburbs. Yann says: "All this work is bound to bear fruit some day." Yann's fellow climber Laurent is tightrope-walking the 20-centimeter-wide wall dividing the concrete promenade behind the tram station from Evry. Behind the wall is a small square – two stories down. "Afraid?" laughs Yann. "Sure, at the edge of a high-rise roof I sometimes get the jitters."

Laurent is clutching the wall, no, he's already let go – he's gone, fallen! But no – his fingers grasp the wall again, and he elegantly jumps down onto the promenade.

"This ain't no circus," Guilain had said. "We're not just big building acrobats." What the Yamakasis have been doing for seven years is expressing their attitude towards life, their will to survive in the concrete jungle of the Parisian suburbs.

"Devour the concrete before it devours you," is their motto. Their name reflects their attitude. In Zairian it means "strong spirit, strong man." Guilain came up with the name; he was born in Zaire. They can prove that they're strong. But when will they make their breakthrough to a great career? "From one day to the next," says Fred, their manager. "Any minute now." Recently, they met the director Luc Besson, and he definitely wants to make a film with them. "That would be the perfect entrée into the movie business." The Yamakasis once wrote to Jackie Chan, the action star from Hong Kong. They want to go as far as he has.

Health Clubs

Espace Vit'Halles

IJ 6 48, rue Rambuteau, 75003; M Rambuteau
Tel: 01 42 77 21 71
Mon. through Fri. 8 am–10 pm, Sat. 10 am–7 pm, Sun. 10 am–4 pm
Visa, Master

This health club was classified as one of the best of its kind in Europe. It has state-of-the-art equipment, and all kinds of aerobics, stretching, and step-dancing courses are offered in two studios. Sauna and hammam provide relaxation afterwards. Price: 1 year 4,450 FF, 1 month 900 FF, 1 day 100 FF, students get a 20% discount.

Companie Bleue

F 8 100, rue du Cherche-Midi, 75006; M Vaneau
Tel: 01 45 44 47 48
C 9 12, rue de l'Eglise, 75015; M Charles-Michels
Tel: 01 40 59 49 10
Mon., Thurs. 9 am–10 pm, Tues., Wed., Fri. 9 am–9 pm, Sat. 9 am–8 pm, Sun. 10 am–6 pm
Visa

Three acrobats with great professional risks: Laurent, Yann, and Guilain (from left to right) have almost no chance of escaping the drudgery of the Parisian suburbs. But they're giving everything they've got to get out

This health club attempts to combine Chinese medicine and bodily awareness with sports and aerobics. It has a Jacuzzi, a hammam, different saunas, and machines for cardiovascular, muscle, and strength training. At the branch in the 15th *arrondissement*, there's a small swimming pool. For more information contact the club (Cherche-Midi), which in addition to long-term memberships offers special rates for people staying a short time in Paris.

Club Quartier Latin

I 8 *19, rue de Pontoise, 75005;* M *Maubert-Mutualité*
Tel: 01 55 42 77 88
www.Pageszoom.com/ clubquartierlatin
Mon. through Fri. 9 am– 12 midnight,/Sat., Sun., 9:30 am–7:30 pm
Visa

Latin: train, see and be seen

There are fitness and equipment rooms on the first and second floors. A trainer is on hand to offer advice. Daily rate: 70 FF, students 60 FF; memberships: 3 months 1,400/1,000 FF. The club has brand-new squash courts which should be reserved in advance. Price for 40 minutes 60/40 FF, year's membership 2,200/1,800 FF.

Gymnasium Institut Cluny

I 8 *90, bd. St.-Germain, 75005;* M *Cluny-La Sorbonne*
Tel: 01 40 46 00 95
Mon. through Fri. 9:30 am–9 pm, Sat. 9:30 am–8 pm, Sun. 11 am–7 pm
Visa, Master

This branch of the big Gymnasium chain is something special. Besides modern training equipment, there are rooms in the basement for body and soul with whirlpools, algae showers, massage showers, algae poultices, shiatsu, lymph drainage massages, anti-cellulite massages, pressotherapy and electro stimulation. Contact the institute to find out about special rates for vacationers. Further addresses:
75003: 62, bd. Sébastopol
Tel: 01 40 46 00 95
75008: 129, bd. Haussmann
Tel: 01 42 89 89 14
75014: 226, bd. Raspail
Tel: 01 43 21 14 40
75018: 60, rue Ordener
Tel: 01 42 51 15 15

Tennis

Gymnase Club Tennis Montparnasse

F 9/10 *25, av. du Capitaine-Dronne, 75014*
M *Montparnasse-Bienvenue*
Tel: 01 43 20 89 00
Mon. through Wed. 9 am– 9 pm, Thurs. through Sat. 9 am–10 pm, Sun. 9 am–8 pm
Visa, Master (starting at 100 FF)

The tennis courts on the roof of the Montparnasse railway station have a real big-city flair. You can bat the ball around on five covered courts. They cost from 70 to 140 FF per hour; reservations are advisable.

Forest Hill

B 11 *Aquaboulevard, 4, rue Louis Armand, 75015*
M *Balard*
Tel: 01 40 60 10 00
Daily 9 am–11 pm, cashier open till 9 pm
Visa, Master

There are nine hard courts (four indoors). A membership is not required. You have to make a reservation. Costs 58 FF for children 11 and under, 78 FF for all others. The staff speaks good English.

Tennis Luxembourg

GH 8 *Jardin du Luxembourg, rue de Vaugirard, 75006;* M *St-Placide RER B Luxembourg Daily 8 am–9 pm Tel: 01 43 25 79 18*

Relaxing games: Jardin du Luxembourg

The six hard outdoor courts are very popular because they're in the middle of a park. After you play, you can relax in one of the little cafés, or on Sundays you can watch one of the numerous chess games being played here. One hour costs 38 FF, till 11 am half that amount.

Squash

Squash Montmartre

H 1 *14, rue Achille Martinet, 75018;* M *Lamarck-Caulaincourt; Tel: 01 42 55 38 30 Mon. through Fri. 10 am–11 pm, Sat., Sun. 10 am–8 pm; Visa*

Four courts. 30 minutes costs 40 FF, a three-month membership 900 FF. Students pay only 28 FF for half an hour (this offer is only valid on weekdays from 10:30 am to 12 noon and from 2:30 pm to 5:30 pm).

Club Quartier Latin

I 8 *19, rue de Pontoise, 75005;* M *Maubert-Mutualité Tel: 01 55 42 77 88 www.Pageszoom.com/ clubquartierlatin Mon. through Fri. 9 am– 12 midnight, Sat., Sun. 9:30 am–7:30 pm Visa*

The dressing rooms and the courts were recently renovated. Four courts; reservations advisable. 60 FF for 40 minutes, 40 FF for students. 1 year membership 2,100/ 1,500 FF, 6 months 1,400/1,000 FF.

Bike Rental

Gepetto et Vélos

I 9 *46, rue Daubenton, 75005;* M *Censier-Daubenton; Tel: 01 43 37 16 17 Tues. through Sun. 9 am– 1 pm, 3 pm–7:30 pm All credit cards*

Gepetto: wheeler-dealers

The staff here speaks English, French, German, and Dutch. Relatively low prices. Wooden and metal toys on sale for children. Bike rental: 75 FF per day, 40 FF per half day, 130 FF for the weekend, 250 FF for a week.

La Maison du Vélo Roue

IJ 6 *95bis, rue Rambuteau, 75001;* M *Les Halles Tel: 01 53 46 43 77 Daily 9 am–7 pm All credit cards*

Located almost in the middle of the city. You can rent a bike all day long and ride to distant *arrondissements* – the best alternative to the métro. All the bikes look new and similar to one another – not original, but practical. Prices: 20 FF for an hour, 50 FF for half a day, 75 FF for a day, 1,000 FF deposit.

Paris à Vélo C'est Sympa

K 8 *37, bd. Bourdon, 75004* M *Bastille Tel: 01 48 87 60 01 Mon. through Fri. 9 am– 1 pm, 2 pm–7 pm, Sat., Sun. 9 am–7 pm Visa, Amex, Master*

You can rent a bike here, or do a bike tour of Paris with a professional guide. Prices: 80 FF for a day, tandems 160 FF.

Bikes for urban tours

Skating

Bike'N Roller

I 8 6, rue St.-Julien-le-
Pauvre, 75005
M St.-Michel/Notre-Dame
Tel: 01 44 07 35 89
Tues. through Sun. 11 am–
1 pm, 2 pm–7:30 pm
Visa, Master

Rentals, sales, and
repairs of blades and
bikes. Right next to
Notre Dame cathedral
– good starting point
for tours of the city
center. Prices: bikes
110 FF for a day 30 FF
for an hour), roller-
blades 80 FF for a day
(30 FF for an hour).

Marathon-Décathlon

I 6 94, rue de Rivoli, 75004
M Châtelet or Hôtel de Ville
Tel: 01 44 54 81 30
Mon. through Sat. 10 am–
7:30 pm; Visa, Master

Besides a rental service
(80 FF per day, 50 FF
per half day including
equipment), courses
are offered, mainly
on Wednesdays and
Saturdays. For more
information contact
the Ecole Française
de Roller (16, rue de
Brantôme, 75003,
Tel: 01 48 87 36 08).

Billiards

Clichy Montmartre

**Quiet days in Clichy:
French billiards**

G 3 Billard Club – Cercle
des Jeux, 84, rue de Clichy,
75009; **M** Pl. de Clichy
Tel: 01 48 78 32 85
Daily 10 am–6 am
No credit cards

Five French billiard
tables, eight American
super-modern 2001
tables, snooker, and
pool. All in a stun-
ningly beautiful
billiard room with
golden, wood-paneled
walls, a big wall mir-
ror, and a mosaic
floor. Nice little bar.
True Parisian flair.
Prices: 100 FF deposit
for cues, billiards
50–75 FF per hour.

A Day at the Races

At the Hippodrome, your betting dreams might just come true.

Horseracing buffs don't believe
in luck. Competence and instinct
are the most important things.
If you want to watch an exciting
race, be in Paris on October 3rd,
when the most important race on
the Hippodrome de Longchamp –
Le Prix de l'Arc de Triomphe –
his held. If you can't be there on
that date, no problem. The season
lasts from August 31 to the end of
October. Admission is 50 FF –
plus any money you wish to bet.

Hippodrome de Longchamp

16e 2, route des Tribunes,
75016 Bois de Boulogne
Tel: 01 44 30 75 00

Inline Parade – Skating Away Every Friday

Boris Elohlavek initiated the inline parade that rolls through Paris every Friday A veritable party for 15,000 skaters

Boris Elohlavek, 28, doesn't know whether he should be happy about the development of his inline parade, or whether he should be upset about the whole thing. Five years ago, when he organized the first parade on wheels, ten people took part. Today, when the weather is good, up to 15,000 Parisians participate – an organizational feat almost too much for one man.

"I spend the whole week preparing for this evening, and sometimes I hate it. But when I'm in the middle of the huge throng, my head is in the clouds."

Paris is grateful and feels the same way. Every Friday (except when it rains), even on holidays such as Good Friday or Christmas, inline freaks meet well before 10 pm at the Place d'Italie in front of the

Billard 2001

L 7 9–11, cour Debille, 75011; **M** *Voltaire*
Tel: 01 43 48 41 75
Mon. through Fri.
12 noon–2 pm,
Sat., Sun. 1 pm–2 am
Visa

Sixteen American tables, three French tables. Bar, brasserie, game and video club. The city magazine Pariscope says it's one of the nicest billiard halls in Paris. Prices: carambolage 55 FF, American 65 FF.

Blue Billard

L 5 111–113, rue St.-Maur, 75011; **M** *Parmentier*
Tel: 01 43 55 87 21
Daily 11 am–2 am
Visa, Master

Blue Billard: blue caps and blue carpeting

Two rooms in over 1,000 square yards of space in a former camera factory with a glass roof. 20 tables. Carambolage (65 FF per hour), American (70 FF), pool (65 FF). Blue carpeting and subdued light.

Piscine des Halles

I 6 Centre Sportif Suzanne Berlioux, 10, pl. de la Rotonde, Forum des Halles, Place Carée, 75001
M *Les Halles*
Tel: 01 42 36 98 44
www.multimania.com/ piscinedeshalles
Mon. 11:30 am–10 pm, Tues., Thurs., Fri. 11:30 am–10 pm, Wed. 10 am–7 pm, Sat. Sun. 9 am–5 pm

Modern swimming pool; a variety of plants creates a pleasant ambience. Price 25 FF, 10-entrance pass 230 FF, 1 hour of training 50 FF, water gymnastics 40 FF.

Club Quartier Latin

I 8 19, rue de Pontoise, 75005
M *Maubert-Mutualité*
Tel: 01 55 42 77 88

Cinéma Gaumont Grand Ecran, have a quick burger at McDonald's, lace up their skates, talk and smoke, and then at 10 sharp set off on a secret route – only the police and the 100-head organizational team know what it is – straight through Paris. "In five years we've never taken the same route," says Boris. "I think by now I've skated down every street in Paris."

J 11 **Meeting spot:** *every Friday at Place d'Italie (last stop on the* **M** *line No. 5), at the Cinéma Gaumont Grand Ecran. Departure: 10 pm. Lasts 2 to 3 hours. Info: Bureau de Tourisme, Tel: 01 49 52 53 14*

Nostalgia and wet rooms: Club Quartier Latin

Due to school swimming courses, the opening times vary; best to call first. The swimming pool, dating back to 1933 and painted light blue and white, is very nostalgic. The pool has six 25-meter lanes and a 1-meter diving board. Prices: 44 FF, 10-entrance pass 360 FF.

Sporting Goods Stores

Go Sport

I 6 *10, rue Boucher, 75001;* **M** *Châtelet Tel: 01 55 34 34 03*
I 6 *Forum des Halles, 75011;* **M** *Les Halles Tel: 01 40 26 40 52*
K 5 *10, pl. de la République, 75001* **M** *République Tel: 01 48 05 71 85 Mon. through Sat. 10 am–7:30 pm All credit cards*

Big sporting goods chain. Wide range of athletic equipment. Relatively cheap. Competent, friendly service.

Décathlon

G 5 *23, bd. de la Madeleine, 75001;* **M** *Madeleine Tel: 01 55 35 97 55 Mon. through Fri. 10 am–8 pm, Sat. 9:30 am–8 pm*

D 3 *26, av. de Wagram, 75008;* **M** *Ternes Tel: 01 45 72 66 88 Mon. through Sat. 10 am–8 pm, Thurs. till 9 pm*
B 11 *4–6, rue Louis Armand 75015;* **M** *Balard Tel: 01 45 55 58 60 45 Mon. through Fri. 10 am–8 pm, Sat. 9:30 am–8 pm, Sun. 10:30 am–7:30 pm Visa, Master*

Sporting goods hypermarket. Specializes in rollerblades, cycling, *randonnée* (hiking + mountain climbing), and fitness. The service (bike, ski, surf, and snowboard workshop) is excellent; bike and rollerblade rentals. (Bicycles: 80 FF for one day, 40 FF for an additional day; mountain bikes: 99 FF for one day, 49 FF for an additional day; inline skates: 60 FF per day).

Femmes Fatales in the Louvre

80 percent of all Paris tourists want to see her: Leonardo da Vinci's Lisa Gioconda

The "Mona Lisa" may be the world's most famous painted lady, but she's by no means the only beautiful woman in the Louvre. The other *femmes fatales* in the museum aren't constantly photographed by tourists or the object of such remarks as "Isn't she beautiful?" As a result, you can spend 15 minutes or so alone with these enticing ladies. Take another painting by Leonardo da Vinci, "La belle Ferronniere." She certainly doesn't look 500 years old. Her expression is more serious than that of the Mona Lisa, but her gaze is no less penetrating. Those who don't like being observed so intensely might prefer to move on to Leonardo's young Mary figures: the "Madonna of the Rocks" and "St.-Anne" only have eyes for the Christ child. A more intimate experience is depicted just steps away from the Mona Lisa by Titian's "Girl in Front of the Mirror."

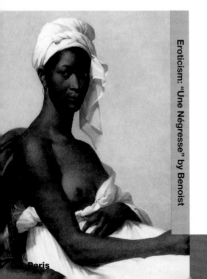

Paris

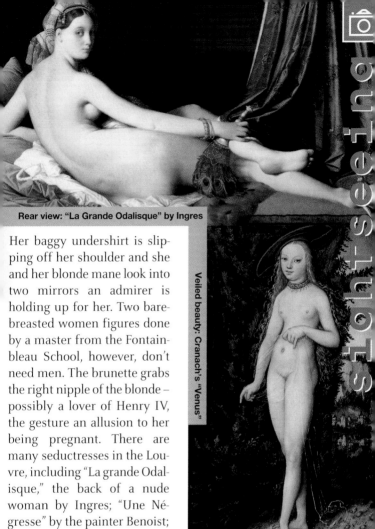

Rear view: "La Grande Odalisque" by Ingres

Veiled beauty: Cranach's "Vénus"

Her baggy undershirt is slipping off her shoulder and she and her blonde mane look into two mirrors an admirer is holding up for her. Two bare-breasted women figures done by a master from the Fontainbleau School, however, don't need men. The brunette grabs the right nipple of the blonde – possibly a lover of Henry IV, the gesture an allusion to her being pregnant. There are many seductresses in the Louvre, including "La grande Odalisque," the back of a nude woman by Ingres; "Une Négresse" by the painter Benoist; or Cranach's "Vénus," clad only in a transparent veil.

Other half-naked heroines show the strength of their gender. Delacroix's "Liberté" from 1830, the epitome of the French nation, leads her people to the barricades. With so many beautiful woman, it's worth standing in line outside the pyramid housing the entrance to the Louvre. The pyramid has just turned ten years old. Since it opened, the number of visitors has nearly doubled.

City Tours

Cityrama

G 6 *4, pl. des Pyramides,
75001;* M *Pyramides
Tel: 01 44 55 61 00
Price: 2 hours 150 FF
Visa, Master, Amex,
Diners*

Outings in comfortable buses. Information is provided via headphones in the language desired (13 are available!).

Touringscope

H 4 *11bis, bd. Haussmann,
75009;* M *Chaussée-d'Antin
or Richelieu-Drouot
Tel: 01 53 34 11 91
Fax: 01 53 34 11 90
Price: 3 hours 150 FF
All credit cards*

A big advantage: you travel through Paris in small groups with an expert travel guide; no recorded information. Reservations required.

L'Open Tour

D 4 *116, av. des Champs-
Elysées, 75008;* M *George V
Prices: 1 day 135 FF,
2-day pass 150 FF
Tickets sold at 35 bus stops*

Discover the city in two days. You can get on and off at over 20 stops. Excellent explanations in English and French. Open-top buses, ideal in the summer.

Churches

Saint-Eustache

I 6 *1, rue Rambuteau,
75001;* M *Les Halles
Tel: 01 42 36 31 05
Daily 9 am–8 pm,
Sun. 9 am–12:30 pm,
2:30 pm–8 pm
Free admission*

Second-largest church in Paris. Gothic structure with Renaissance décor, built from 1532 to 1637. Interesting mixture of styles seldom found in this form. You can see the city's most famous organ here.

Cathédrale de Notre Dame

I 7 *Pl. du Parvis Notre-
Dame, 75004;* M *Cité
Tel: 01 42 34 56 10
Daily. 8 am–7 pm
(Sat. closed from
12:30 pm–2 pm)
Free admission*

Parc de la Villette

Parc de la Villette is the biggest park in Paris. It has little in common with the city's idyllic little parks. In Parc de la Villette, formerly the site of a fish market, forward-looking research is carried out. In the middle of the park is the Cité des Sciences et de l'Industrie, where you can view a submarine and learn about various aspects of science. Next to it is the Géode, a large silver ball which houses a 3D movie theater with a 3,600-square-foot screen, called the Cinaxe (a dynamic simulation cinema); then there's the Cité de la Musique, the Grande Halle (with exhibitions), a theater, and the Canal de l'Ourcq, which divides the park in the middle.

19e 75019; M *Pte de Pantin, Pte de la Villette Cité de Sciences et de l'Industrie;
Tel: 01 40 05 80 00 and 01 40 05 12 12; www.cite-sciences.fr; Tues. through Sun. 10 am–7 pm;
price: 50 FF; Géode: hourly films 10 am– 9 pm, English-language headphone translation
included in the price; price: 57 FF, reduced rate 44 FF; Cinaxe: hourly films 11 am–6 pm;
price: 34 FF, reduced rate 29 FF, Techno cite 25 FF, Argonaute submarine 25 FF*

The cathedral on the Ile de la Cité, begun in 1163 and finished in 1345, was one of the first Gothic cathedrals to be built and its towers command a magnificent view

A nice outlook: Notre Dame cathedral

Sainte-Chapelle

I 7 *4, bd. du Palais, 75001*
M *Cité or St.-Michel or Châtelet; Tel: 01 53 73 78 51*
Daily 9:30 am–6:30 pm (April through September), 10 am–5 pm (October through March)
Entrance fee: 35 FF, reduced 23 FF

This church is famous not only for its large, colorful stained-glass windows, but also for its holy relics. On the altar, in a golden vessel, is a piece of Christ's crown of thorns.

Saint-Julien-le-Pauvre

I 8 *1, rue St.-Julien-le-Pauvre, 75005*
M *St.-Michel*
Tel: 01 43 54 52 16
Daily 10 am–7:30 pm
Free admission

This small monastery church built by Benedictine monks around 1170 is the oldest university church in Paris. Today it's the house of prayer of the Greek-Orthodox community.

Panthéon

I 9 *Pl. du Panthéon, 75005;*
M *Luxembourg*
Tel: 01 44 32 18 00
Daily 10 am–5:30 pm (October to March), 9:30 am–6:30 pm (April through September)
Admission: 35 FF, reduced 23 FF

A domed construction completed in 1789, the year of the French Revolution. The church was originally dedicated to St.-Genoveva and was declared a temple of glory for celebrated Frenchmen. The tombs of Voltaire, Rousseau, Victor Hugo, and Emile Zola, among others, are located here.

Saint-Sulpice

G 8 *Pl. St.-Sulpice, 9, rue de Mézières, 75006*
M *St.-Sulpice*
Tel: 01 46 33 21 78
Daily 8:30 am–7:30 pm
Free admission

Renaissance church with frescoes by Delacroix. The little square with the big fountain in front of the church is very lively and romantic. The park benches under the chestnut trees are a nice place to take a break.

Saint-Eugène

I 4 *4, rue du Conservatoire, 75009;* **M** *Grands Boulevards*
Tel: 01 48 24 70 25
Open for masses: Mon. 7 pm, Tues. through Fri. 7:30 am, 12:15 pm, 7 pm, Sat. 10 am, 11:15 am, 6 pm
Free admission

Bland on the outside, beautiful inside. You'd never expect by looking at the exterior that inside is a room that looks more like a colorful festival hall than a church. The architect Boileau, inspired by the décor of Sainte Chapelle, built his first steel church here.

Basilique du Sacré-Cœur

H 2 *Place-du-Sacré-Cœur, 75018;* **M** *Anvers*
Tel: 01 53 41 89 00
Daily 6:15 am–11 pm, crypt and dome: daily 9 am–6 pm
Admission 15 FF, reduced 8 FF

White basilica in Montmartre. The architect who designed this construction was Paul Abaclie (1812–1884). Today it's the main attraction of Montmartre hill. The church is not particularly thrilling inside, but the view from the city's highest hill (138 yards) is fantastic.

City Walks

From the Marais district to the Bastille

The starting point is Place de **l'Hôtel de Ville**, where heads rolled during the French Revolution. Head down the quais de l'Hôtel de Ville to the left, and then turn left onto rue des Barres. The classical façade of **Saint-Gervais** beckons you to enter. Head down rue du Grenier-sur-l'Eau to the **Mémorial du Martyr**, where there is a crypt with the grave of an unknown Jewish martyr. The ocumentation center here is the biggest research center on Judaism in Europe. Turn right onto rue Geoffroy and go down rue de l'Hôtel de Ville, which leads to the **Hôtel de Sens**, a castle-like building in a flamboyant style today housing the **Bibliothèque Forney**. Go up the rue de Fauconnier, turn left onto the rue

Charlemagne, then right again onto rue du Prévôt. Here you can step inside the **Saint-Paul-Saint-Louis**, a Jesuit church built in 1627. Via rue Malher you will reach a part of the district with many small shops and cafés. Signs show the way to various **museums – Musée Picasso, Musée Carnavalet**, etc. If you want to continue toward the Bastille, turn right from rue Malher onto rue des Francs-Bourgeois and keep walking straight ahead to **Place des Vosges**, one of the most beautiful squares in Paris.

From Beaubourg/ Les Halles to the Marais

From the **Centre Georges Pompidou**, the famous art center, you pass the exotic **fountain** with water-spitting machines by Tinguely and colorful figures by Nicky de Saint-Phalle on the

way to the **Eglise Saint-Merri**. Go down rue de la Verrerie toward the Marais, and turn left onto rue des Archives. Numbers 22 to 26 house the **Cloître des Billettes**, the last medieval monastery in Paris, built in 1427. From here you can walk down rue des Francs-Bourgeois into the heart of the Marais (see above).

Saint-Germain

Starting point: M Saint-Germain-des-Prés. From here go down rue Bonaparte, the site of the **Ecole des Beaux-Arts**. Via the Quai Malaquais, you will reach the **Institut de France**. After having a look at the **Pont des Arts**, stroll down rue de Seine, lined with art galleries.

Parks

Jardin du Luxembourg

H 8 *Bd. St.-Michel, 75006*
RER *Luxembourg*
Tel: 01 42 34 20 00
March through November
7:30 am to dusk, December
through February
8:30 am to dusk
Free admission,
playground 10 FF

**Jardin du Luxembourg:
the students' park**

For generations this park has been frequented by students. If the park's standard attractions aren't enough for you, you can sail wooden sailboats in a pool, take your children to the adventure playground, or check out the marionette theater (Tel: 01 43 26 46 47). Plus there a pony walks, beekeeping courses (Tel: 01 42 34 20 00), and beautiful fruit trees.

Parc Montsouris

14ᵉ *Bd. Jourdan, 75014*
M *Pte d'Orléans*
Tel: 01 45 88 28 60
Daily 7:30 am–7 pm
Free admission

English-style park, designed by the landscape architect Adolphe Alphand at the end of the 19th century under Napoléon III. Great lawns, 100-year-old trees, and a lake. The Montsouris is the city's second biggest park and home to the Paris' weather station.

Parc André Citroën

AB 9 *Quai André*
Citroën/rue Balard, 75015
M *Javel or Balard*
Tel: 01 45 57 13 35
Mon. through Fri.
7:30 am to dusk,
Sat., Sun. from 9 am
Dogs, bikes, ball games
prohibited
Free admission

**Water art: Parc André
Citroën is bubbling with
life**

This park on the Seine is modern and playful. The landscape gardeners Provost and Clément play with water, stone, and plants. In the northern section is the *Jardin en Mouvement*, wild terrain, perfect for walks. In the southern part is the *Jardin Noir*, the black park, with dense, dark-colored vegetation.

La Coulée Verte

K 7, L 8, M 9 *Pl. de la*
Bastille to Square
Charles- Péguy,
75012
M *Bastille*

The name means "green run", an apt description of this green artery running through the 12th *arrondissement*. You can take a nice, airy stroll along the Viaduc de la Bastille and look in the arcades and studios.

Parc des Buttes-Chaumont

M 3 *Rue Manin/Rue de*
Crimée, 75019
M *Buttes-Chaumont*

This grassy 60-acre park also owes its origins to Napoléon III and Adolphe Alphand. Alphand worked on it from 1864 to 1867. The craters and hollows, some of which were done in plaster, must have involved a lot of labor.

**A picturesque park:
Buttes-Chaumont**

1. A lot of ballyhoo at the Disney Parade
2. Big Thunder Mountain, an abandoned goldmine

From Mickey to Merlin

Where you can shrink to the size of a tin soldier

A typical day at Disneyland Paris. In the "Honey, I shrunk the audience" 3D cinema, the spectators scream. And they scream often here. For example, when they're shrunk to the size of tin soldiers, or when a giant sneezing dog gives them a shower.

Next door, at "Space Mountain," a cannon is lit that shoots visitors to the moon in 1.8 seconds. If that's too much excitement for you, you might want to watch the Mulan show.

But the true highlight for the 60,000 or so daily visitors is the parade down Main Street featuring Mickey Mouse, Goofy, and Balu. They plunge into a sea of wet kisses, stroking hands, clicking cameras, and open notebooks.

How to get there

Disneyland is located 32 kilometers east of Paris. Take the A4 interstate, get off at the Metz/Nancy exit, and then take exit 14 (Val d'Europe/Parc Disneyland).

The details

The park is open from 9 am to 11 pm, as of September it closes at 8 pm. From April through October adults pay 220 FF and children 11 or under 170 FF. More info at: www.disney.de.

Jardin des Tuileries

G 6 *Pl. de la Concorde, 75001;* M *Concorde*
Tel: 01 49 26 07 59
Daily 7:30 am–9 pm
Free admission

Classical park in the city center. Popular attraction. A hop, skip, and jump from the Champs-Elysées, with the Louvre in the background; you can see the Orangerie and visit the Jeu de Paume museum. There's an old carousel and a pool for little boats.

Tuileries: the Orangerie is a main attraction in Paris

Bike Tours

Cyclistes Randonneurs FFCT

F 10/11 *32, rue Raymond Losserand, 75015*
M *Pernety*
Tel: 01 34 16 07 41
Fax: 01 43 35 14 06
E-Mail: mdb.idf@club-internet.fr
Regular meetings:
Wed. 6 pm–7:30 pm; Visa

Regular bike trips to outlying areas (25–75 miles). Bring your own bike to the train station, pack a picnic lunch, and spend an enjoyable day with others.

Paris-Vélo

IJ 10 *2, rue du Fer-à-Moulin, 75005*
M *Censier-Daubenton*
Tel: 01 43 37 59 22
Daily 10 am–7 pm
Bike rental: 90 FF
City tours: 120–180 FF
Visa

Bike rentals, guided group city tours on weekends and Wednesday evenings. Reservations are required for the group tours. Ask about the schedule.

Boat Trips

Bateaux-Vedettes du Pont-Neuf

H 7 *Square du Vert-Galant, 75001;* **M** *Pont-Neuf*
Tel: 01 46 33 98 38
Daily 10:30 am, 11:15 am, 12 noon; half-hour trips from 1:30 pm to 6:30 pm, and from 9 pm to 10:30 pm
Price: 50 FF, 12 and younger 25 FF, groups (at least 20 people) 20 FF
1 hour long
Visa, Master

The trip affords views of numerous monuments in Paris. Information in French and English. The boats are decorated with garlands of flowers. You can buy a photo of yourself taken at the beginning of the trip.

Bateaux-Mouches

D 6 *Pont de l'Alma, 75016*
M *Alma-Marceau*
Tel: 01 40 76 99 99
Tel: 01 42 25 96 10 (reservations)
Price: 1 hour 40 FF
Daily 10:30 am, 11 am, 11:30 am, 12:15 pm, 2 pm, 2:30 pm, and 3:15 pm; thereafter every 20 to 30 minutes till 10 pm; explanations in four languages; trips with lunch (reservations required): Sat., Sun., and holidays at 1 pm; 1 hour 45 minutes long; price: 300 FF, 12 and under 150 FF
Visa, Master, Amex, Diners

Classic Seine trip; the most famous boat excursion in Paris. The mooring is near the Eiffel Tower. Great on sunny days, because above the glass house, which keeps you dry when it rains, is a roof with seats in the open air.

Canauxrama

K 3, L 2 *13, quai de la Loire, 75019;* **M** *Jaurès*
Tel: 01 42 39 15 00
Price: 80 FF, reduced 60 FF, no reduced prices on weekends
Leaves at 9:45 am and 2:30 pm from Port de l'Arsenal (12th arr.)
M *Bastille; 9:30 am and 2:45 pm from the Bassin de la Villette*
M *Jaurès*
Visa, Master

The canal trip leads through underground vaults, then through the lock of the Canal St.-Martin. Lasts three hours.

Canauxrama: the grand canals of Paris

Helicopter Flights

Above the clouds...

Aéroport *Aéroport de Paris Le Bouquet;* **RER** *B, Bus 350*
Tel: 01 48 05 30 48
Price: 800 FF per person
Flying time 25 minutes
Reservations at Fnac and the Office de Tourisme de Paris
All credit cards

A dream come true. A 50-mile helicopter ride over Paris.

Hamburg from above: the Hotel Atlantic on the water offers more than excellent accommodation

Hamburg celebrates: bars are springing up everywhere

Hamburg's soul: the harbor is a workplace, outing destination, trendy going-out area, and much more

Hamburg goes shopping: a wide variety of stores in a small area

Hamburg politics: in the town hall the city's future is being mapped out

Hamburg is ...!

MAX CITY GUIDE visits the city in its own backyard, where MAX is head-quartered.

Hamburg, Germany, is the city in question. We dismiss the clichés (the people of Hamburg are arrogant and stodgy) and show a young, lively metropolis that's constantly undergoing exciting changes. Hamburg is on the water. So we wish you smooth sailing through the next MAX CITY GUIDE!

In bookstores in March 2000

Credits + Publishing

Publisher: te Neues Publishing
Editor-in-chef: Anke Degenhard
Art Director: Kerstin Peters
Director of photography: Kerstin Richter
Editors: Christoph Becker (Manager), Dirk Krömer
Authors: Peter Lau, Astrid Mayer, Nils Minkmar, Stéfan Picker-Dressel, Tanja Requardt, Jürgen Sorges, Frédéric Ulferts, Kia Vahland, Helmut Ziegler
Editorial staff for this edition: Burke Barrett (Translation), Christiane Blass (Managing editor), Jonell Galloway (Text editor)

Editorial staff in Paris: Cristina De La Muela, Bettina Krauss, Jörg Lehmann (Fotos)
Design: Barbara Sullivan, Christian Bretter, Notburga Stelzer
Support work: AKW, Nicole Kleinfeld, Anne-Gael Le Clec'h, Kurt Ritter, Marcus Rothe, Melina Schmidt, Nicolette Thüll, Katrin Viellieber, Markus Weber
Editorial address: MAX CITY GUIDE Milchstraße 1, 20148 Hamburg
Publisher's address: te Neues Publishing 16 West 22nd Street, New York, NY 10010 Tel: (212) 627-9090, Fax: (212) 627-9511 e-mail: tnp@teneues-usa.com www.teneues.com

MAX CITY GUIDE is a trademark of the MAX Verlag GmbH & Co. KG. The paperback edition of Max City Guide in English is a licensed edition of the German magazine Max City Guide, published by agreement between Max Verlag GmbH & Co. KG, a division of the publishing group Milchstrasse, Milchstr. 1, 20148 Hamburg/Germany Publishing Company te Neues.

While we strive for utmost precision in every detail, we cannot be held responsible for any inaccuracies, nor for any subsequent loss or damage arising.

te Neues
www.teneues.com

index

index

The Max City Guides
also available as calendars

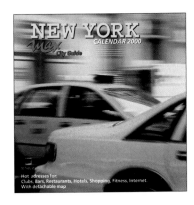

WALL CALENDARS

Size 30 x 30 cm

New York
ISBN: 3-8238-**3579**-3

London
ISBN: 3-8238-**3580**-7

Berlin
ISBN: 3-8238-**3581**-5

$12.99   c$19.50   £ 4.99

Hot addresses for:
Clubs, Bars, Restaurants,
Hotels, Shopping,
Fitness, Internet.
With detachable map.

DELUXE DIARIES

Size 16,5 x 21,6 cm

New York
ISBN: 3-8238-**3696**-X

London
ISBN: 3-8238-**3697**-8

Berlin
ISBN: 3-8238-**3698**-6

$13.99   c$21.00   £ 4.99

London

max
City Guide

te Neues

London at a Glance • City Map and Subway Map

Cool Guides to Hot Cities

London

**Over 400 Current Addresses: The Hottest Clubs
The Coolest Bars • The Cheapest Hotels
The Best Restaurants • The Latest Shopping Tips**

ISBN 3-8238-**9402**-1
now available

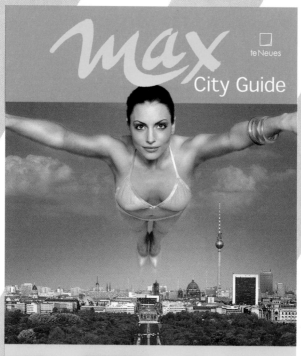